MAN

Photo Anthology / Peter Slater

male/meɪl/adjectiveadjective: maleof or denoting the sex that produces gametes, especially spermatozoa, with which a female may be fertilized or inseminated to produce offspring."male children"synonyms:masculine, to do with men, he-; virile, manly, macho, red-blooded"male sexual behaviour"man, adult male, gentleman;boy, lad, schoolboy, youth, young man, young fellow;laddie;informalguy, fellow, geezer, gent, mother's son;informalbloke, chap, lad;informaldude, bozo, hombre;informaldigger;informaloke, ou, oom;informaladmi;informalbodach;informalcove;archaiccarl"the driver was a burly male in his forties"antonyms:femalerelating to or characteristic of men or male animals."a deep male voice"(of a plant or flower) bearing stamens but lacking functional pistils.(of a fitting or part of machinery) manufactured to fit inside a corresponding female part."the valve has standard half-inch threaded male ends"nounnoun: male; plural noun: malesa male person, plant, or animal."the audience consisted of adult males"

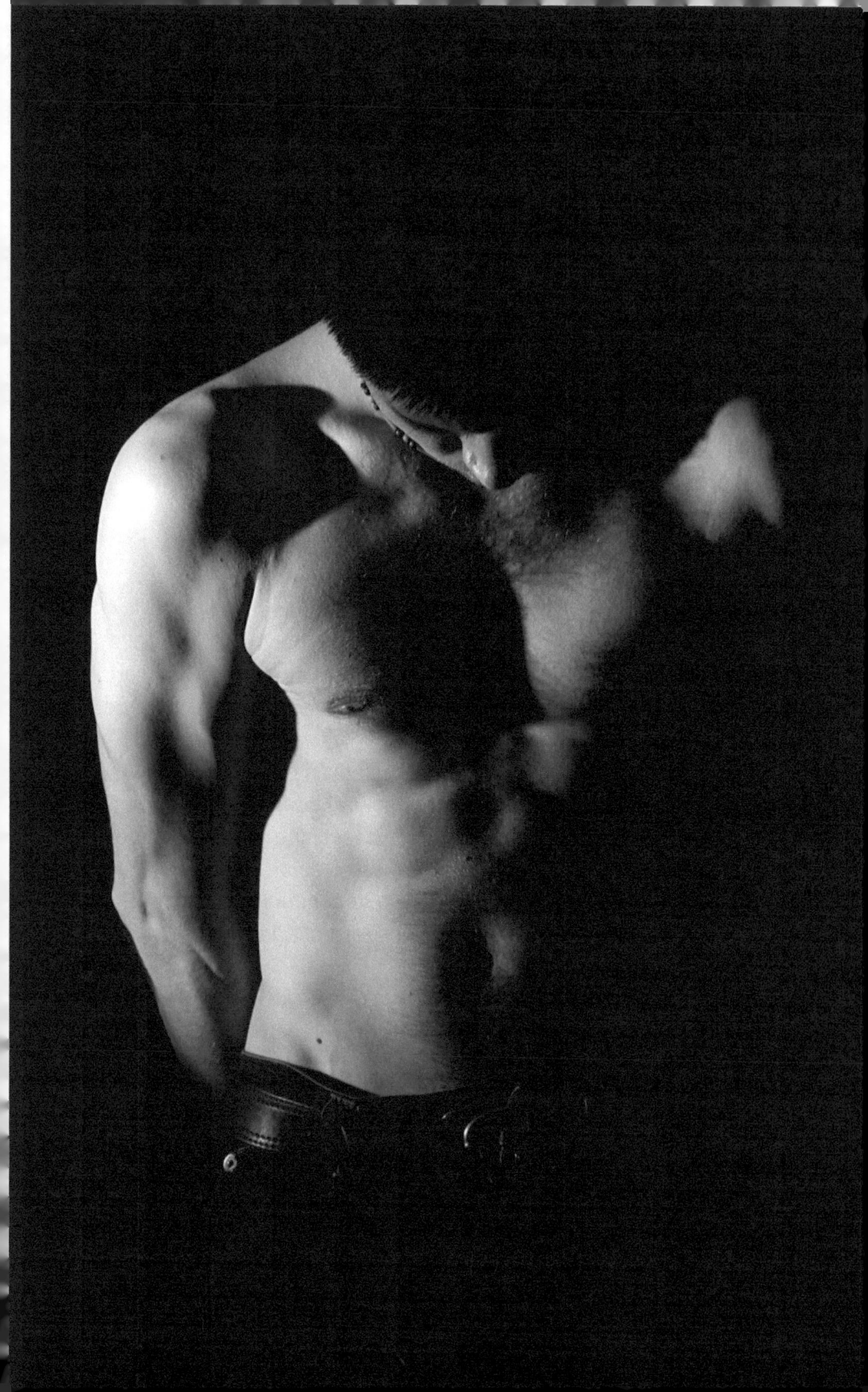

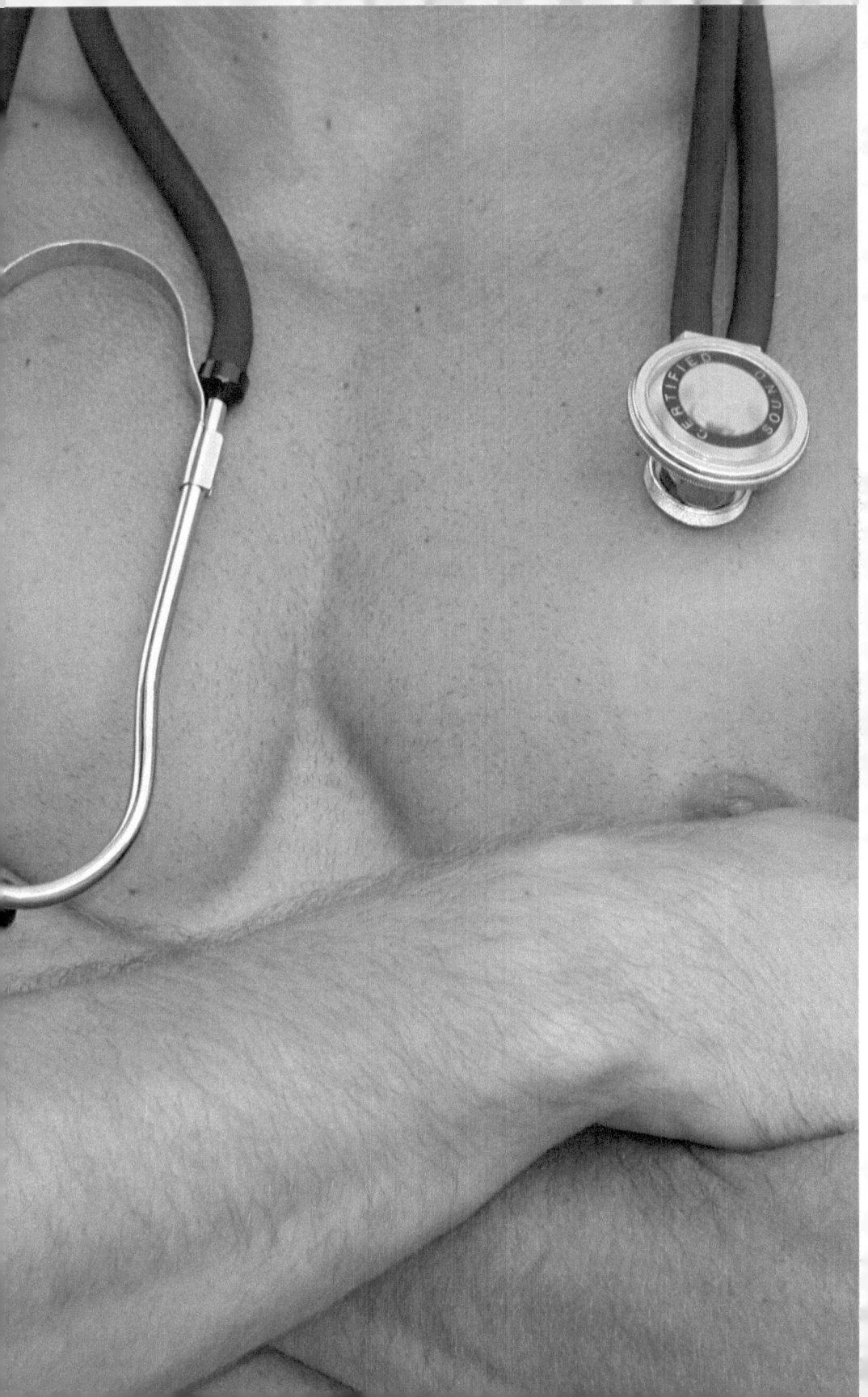

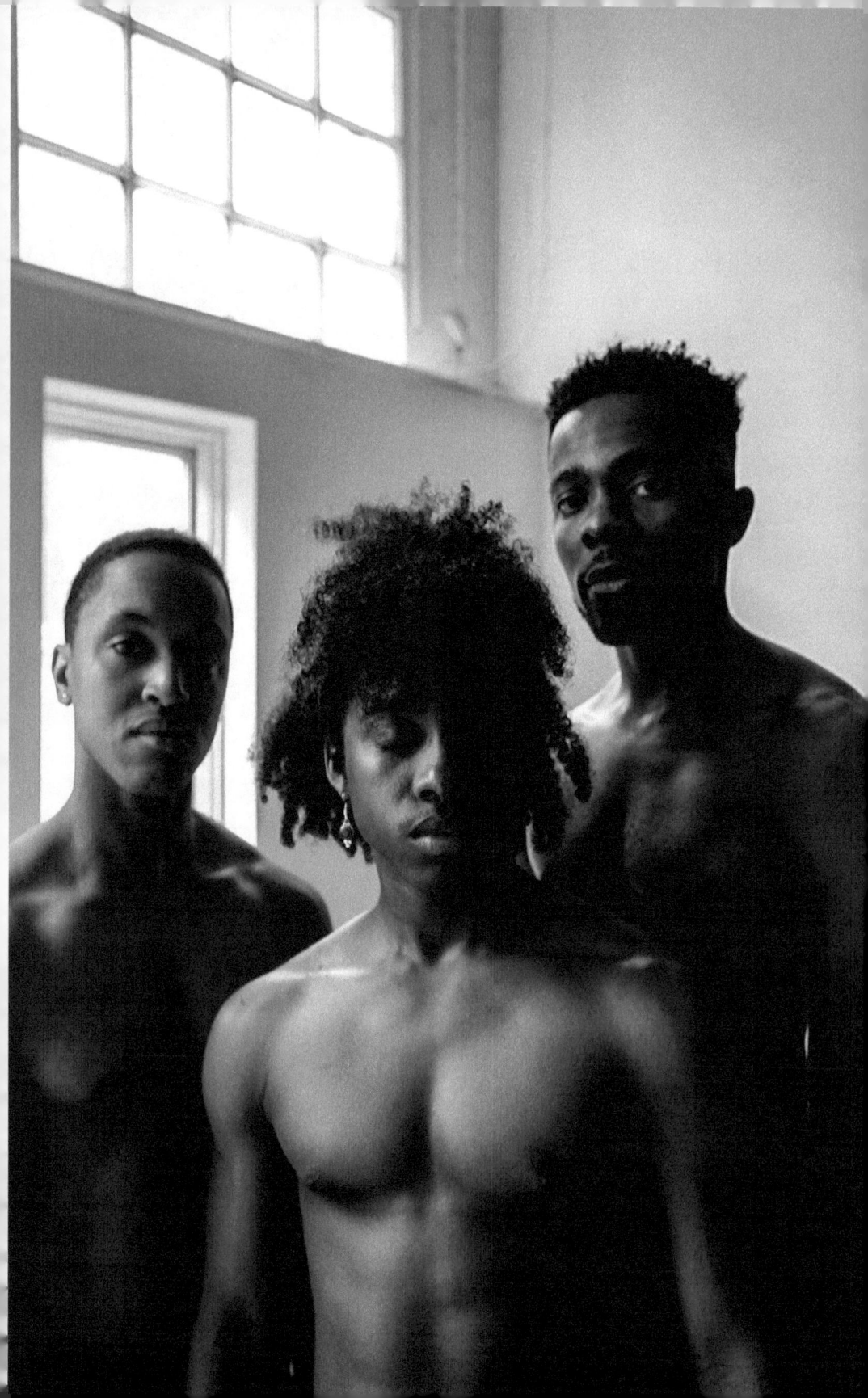

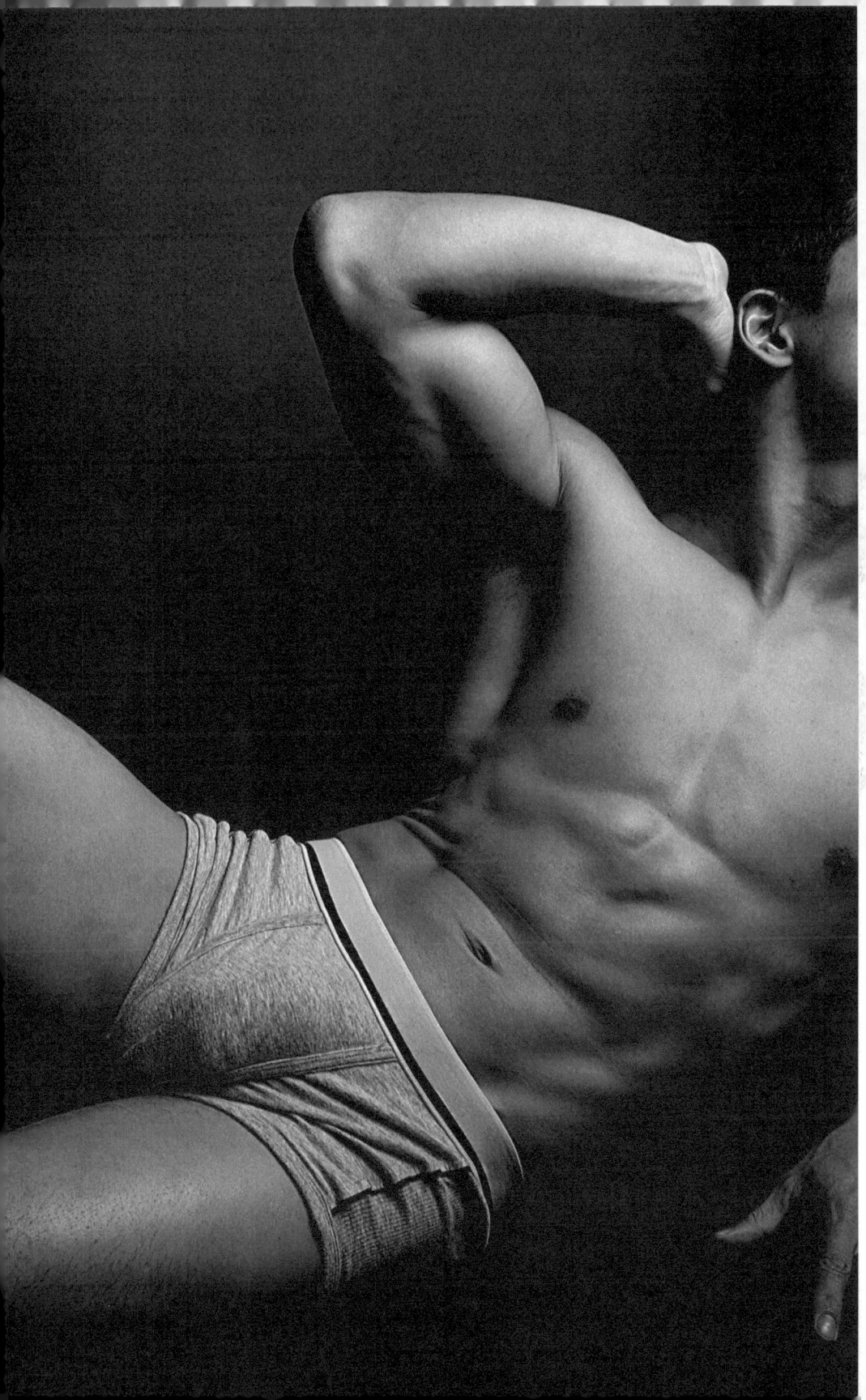

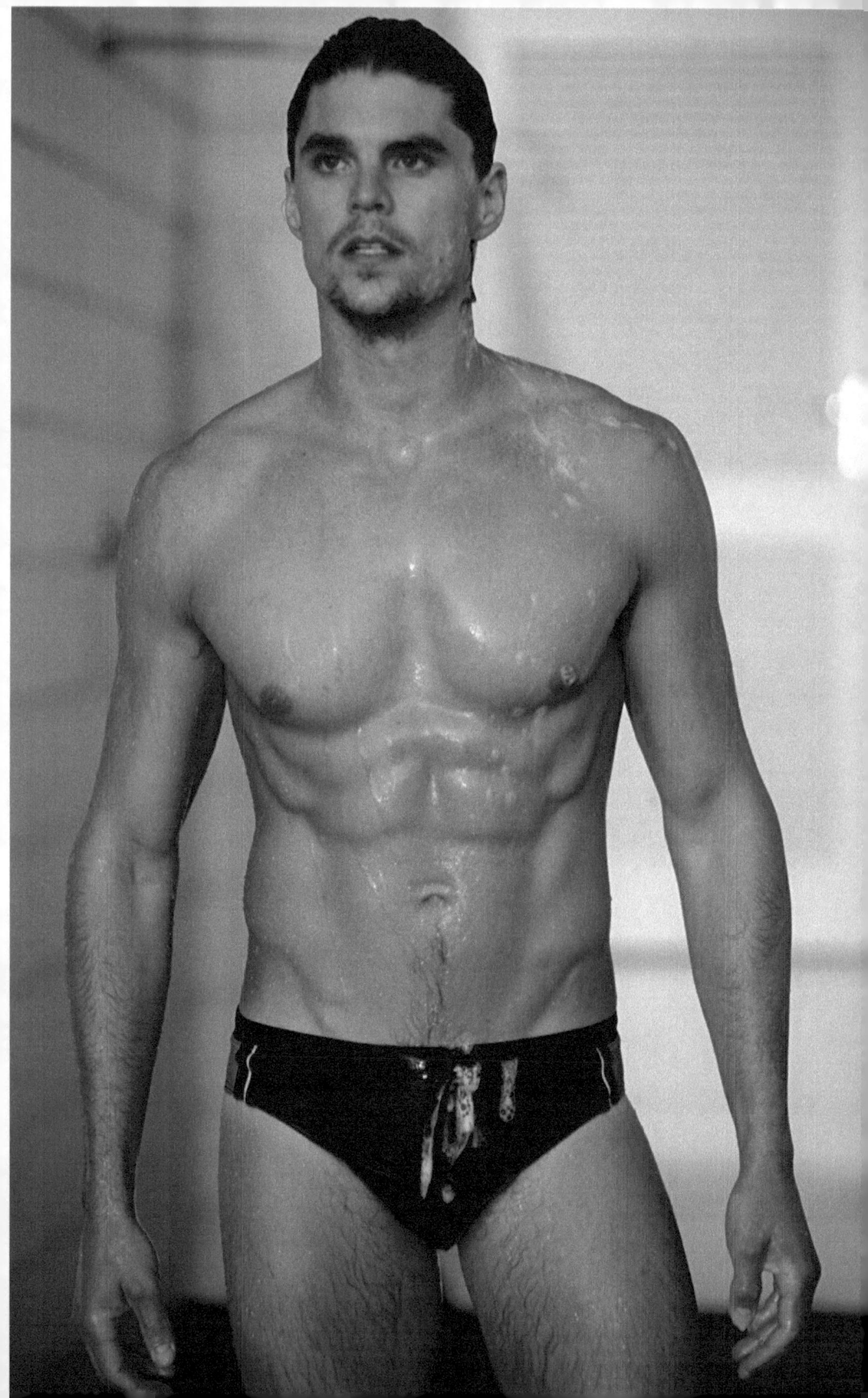

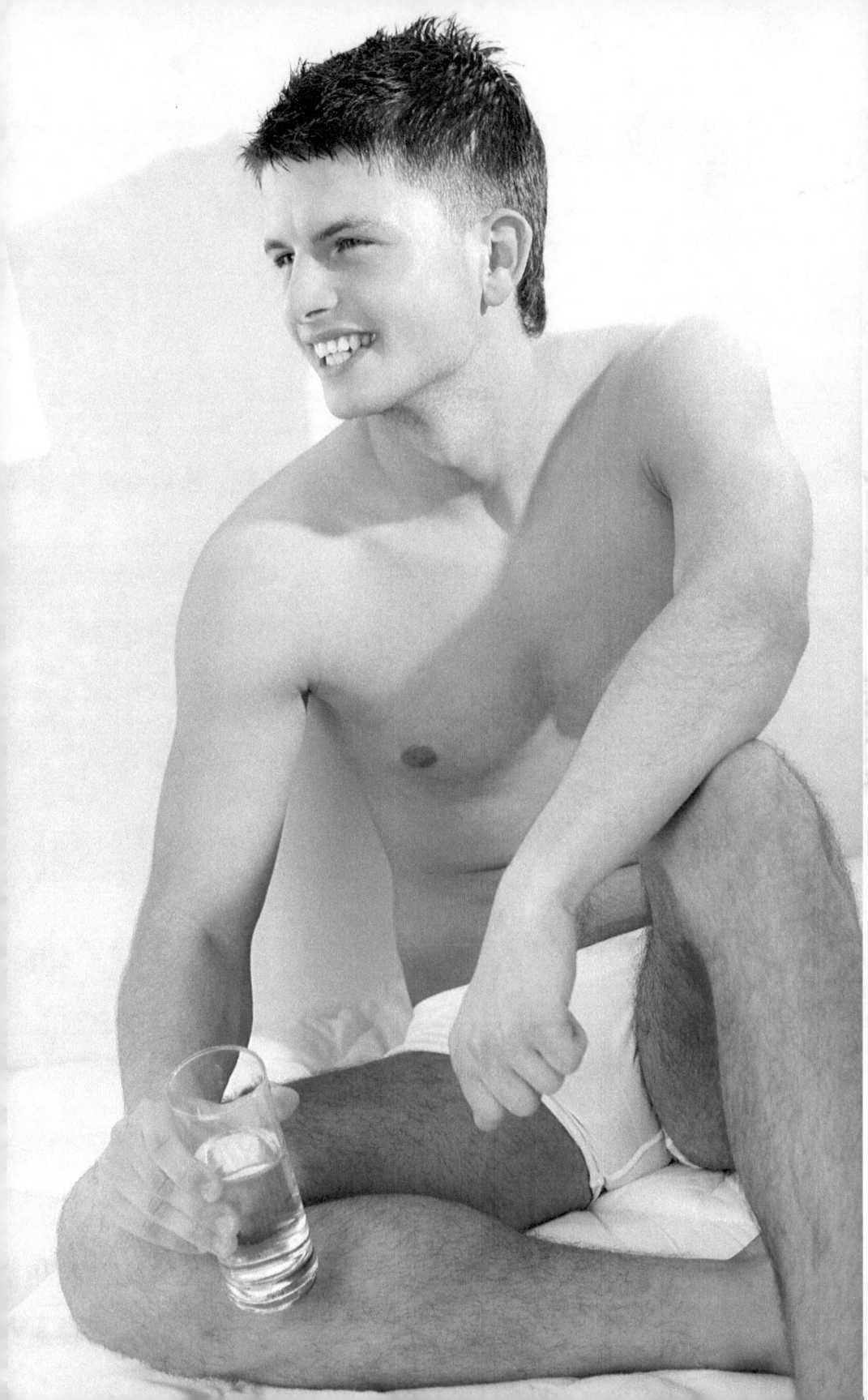

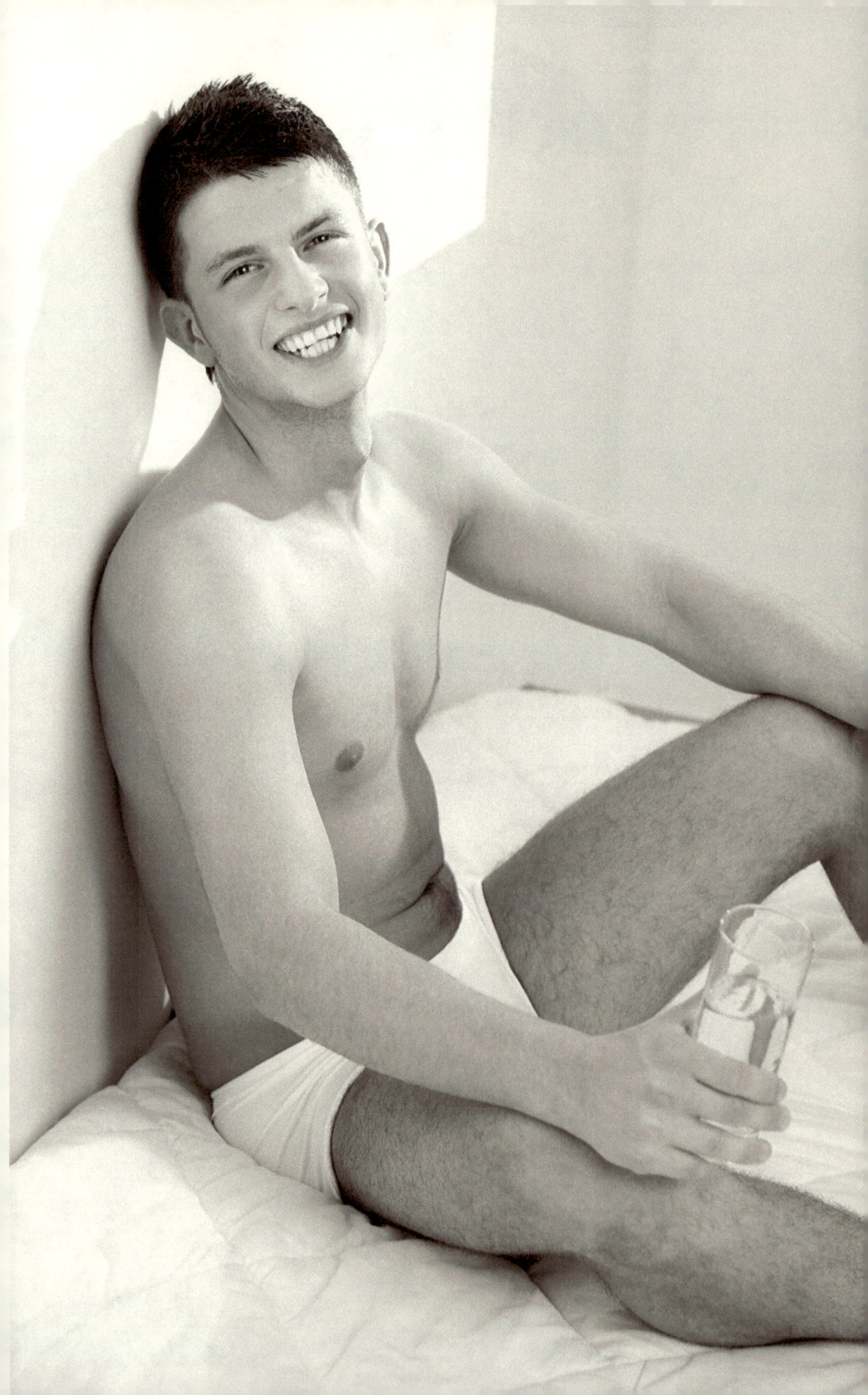

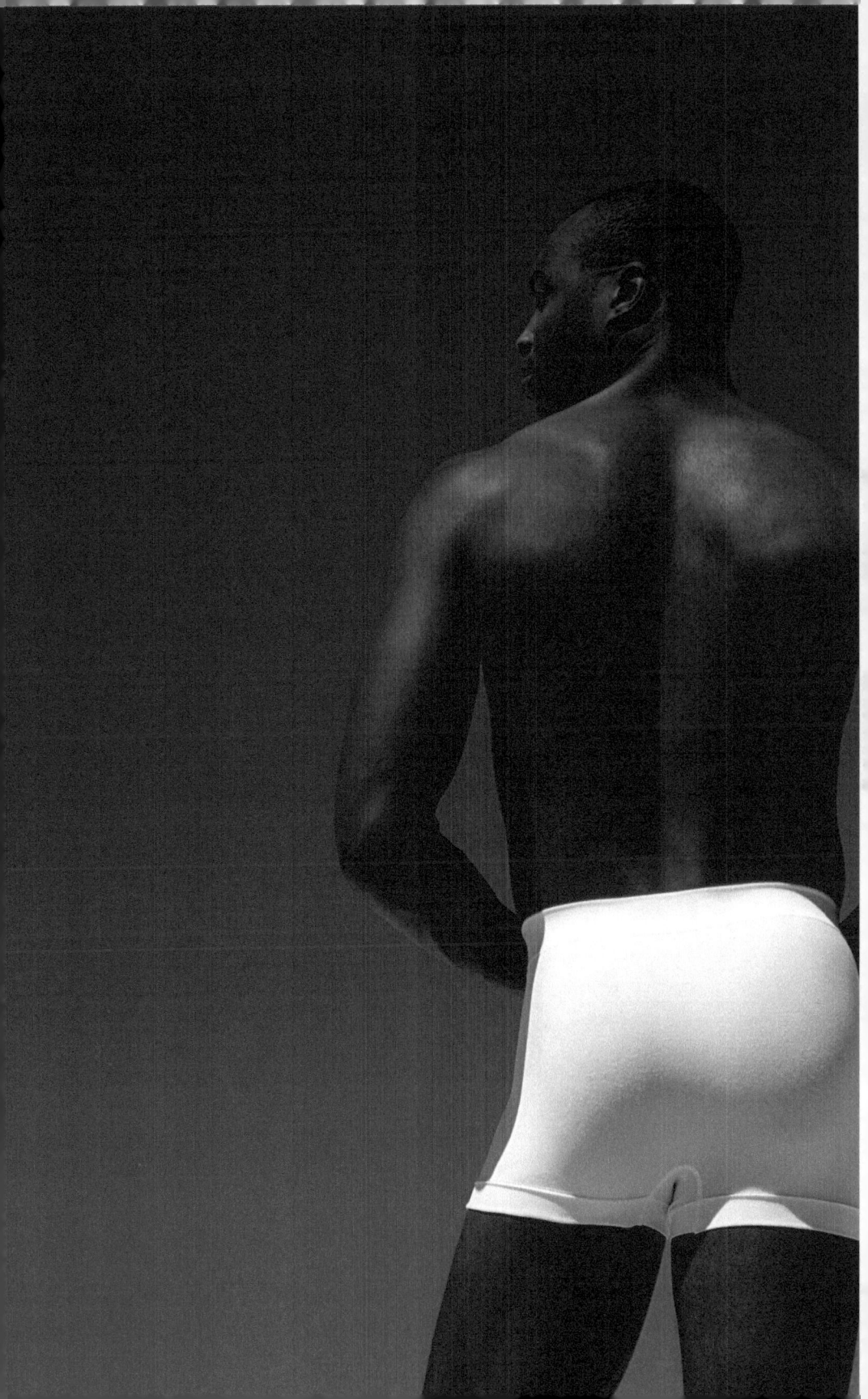

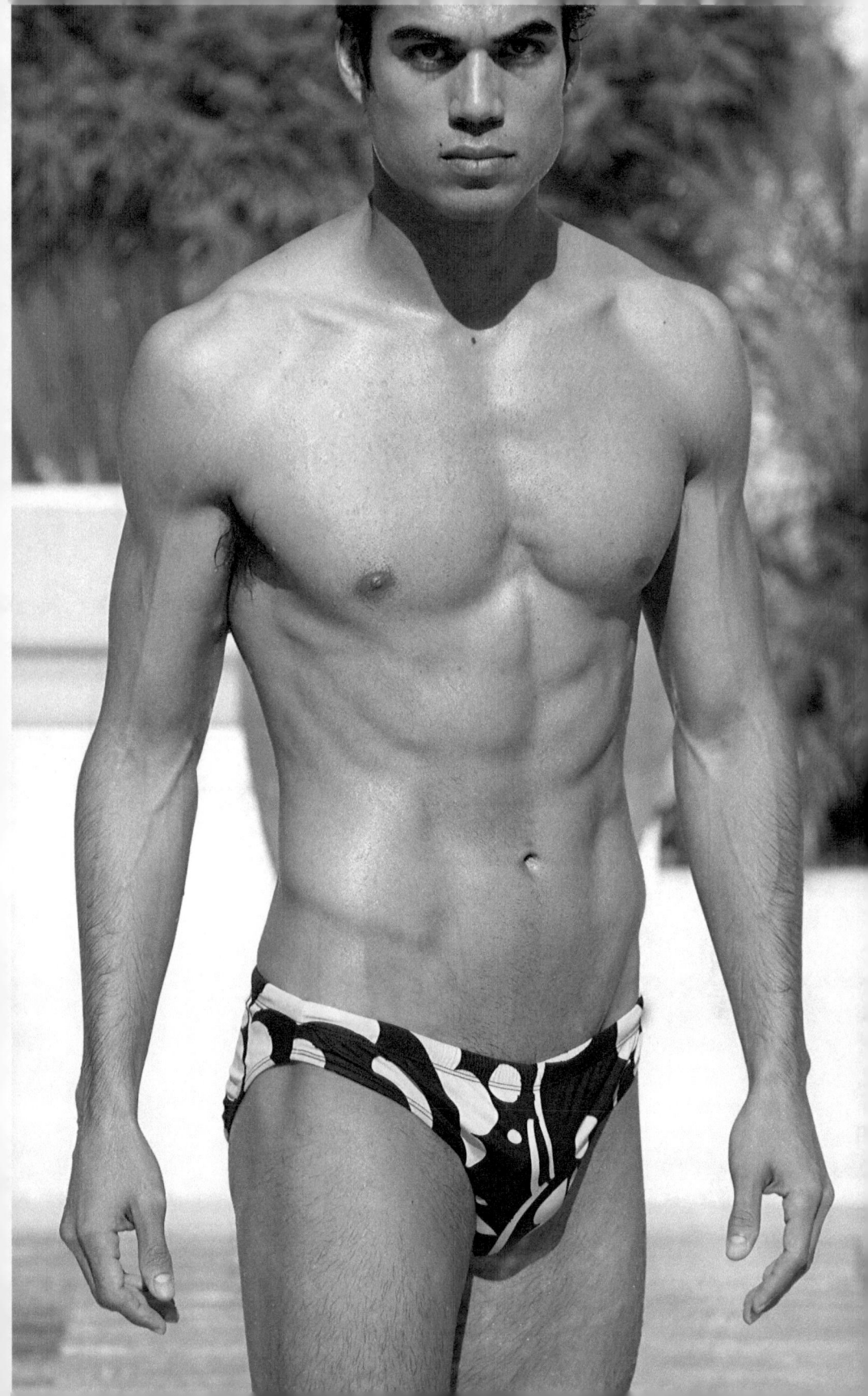

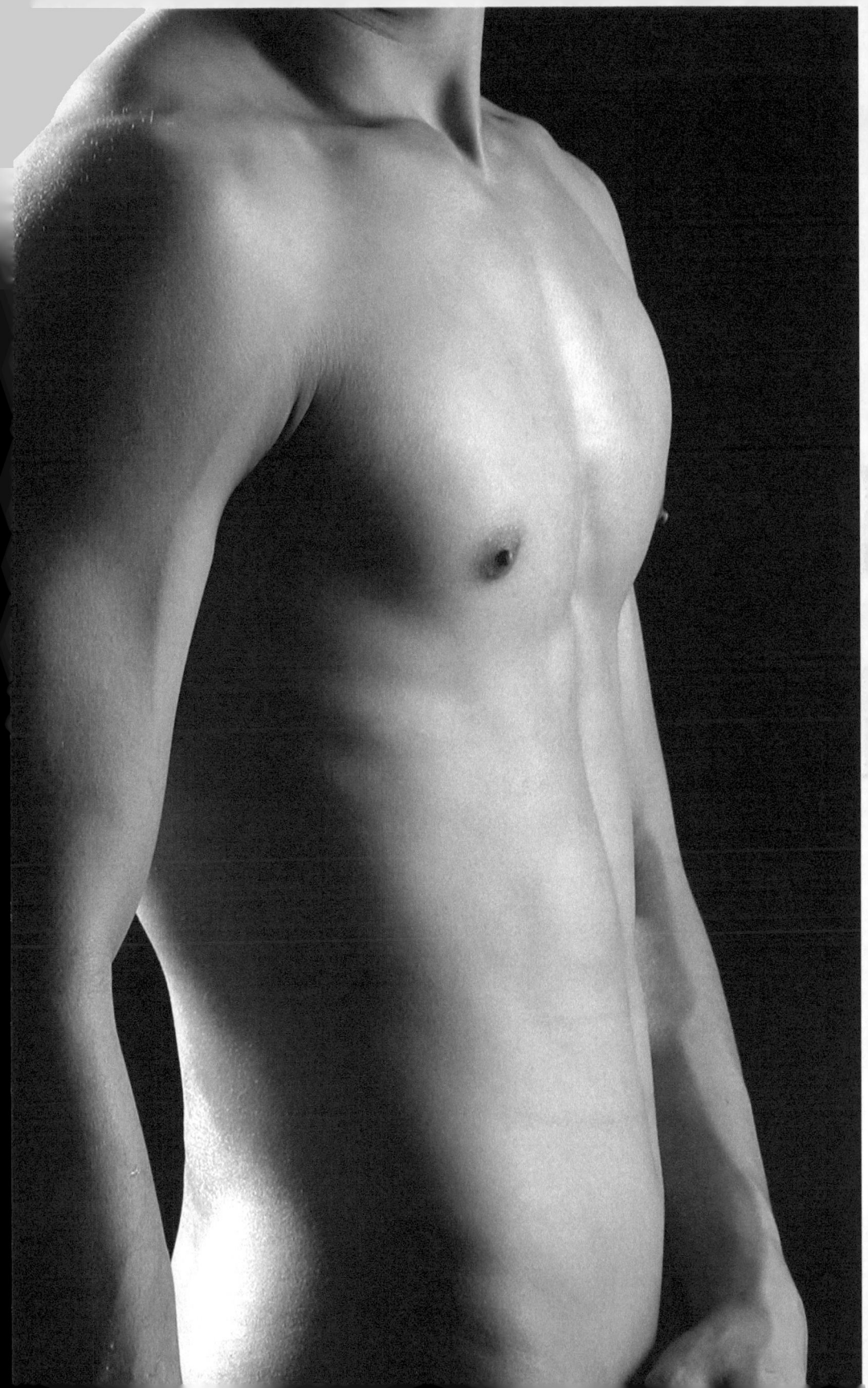

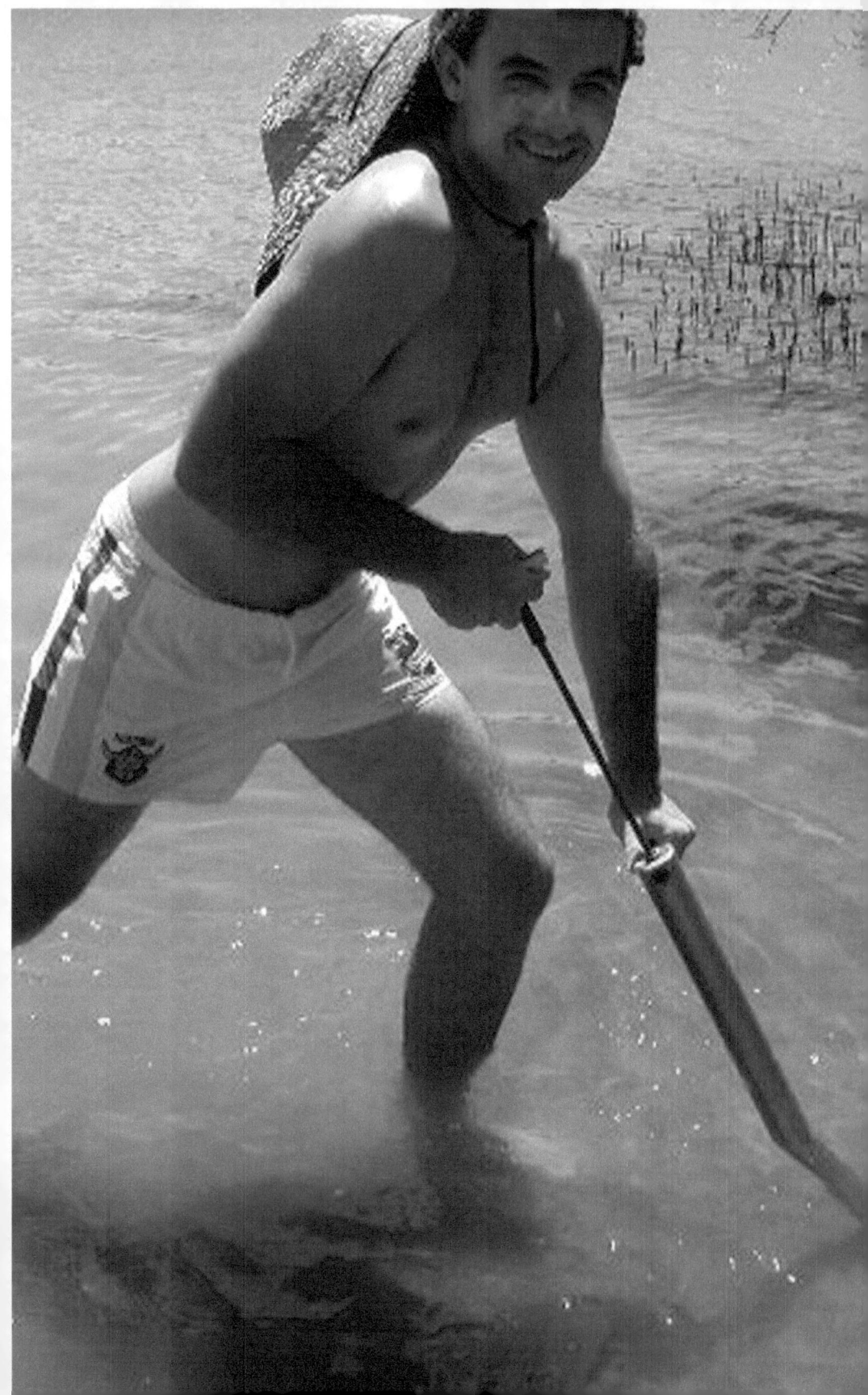

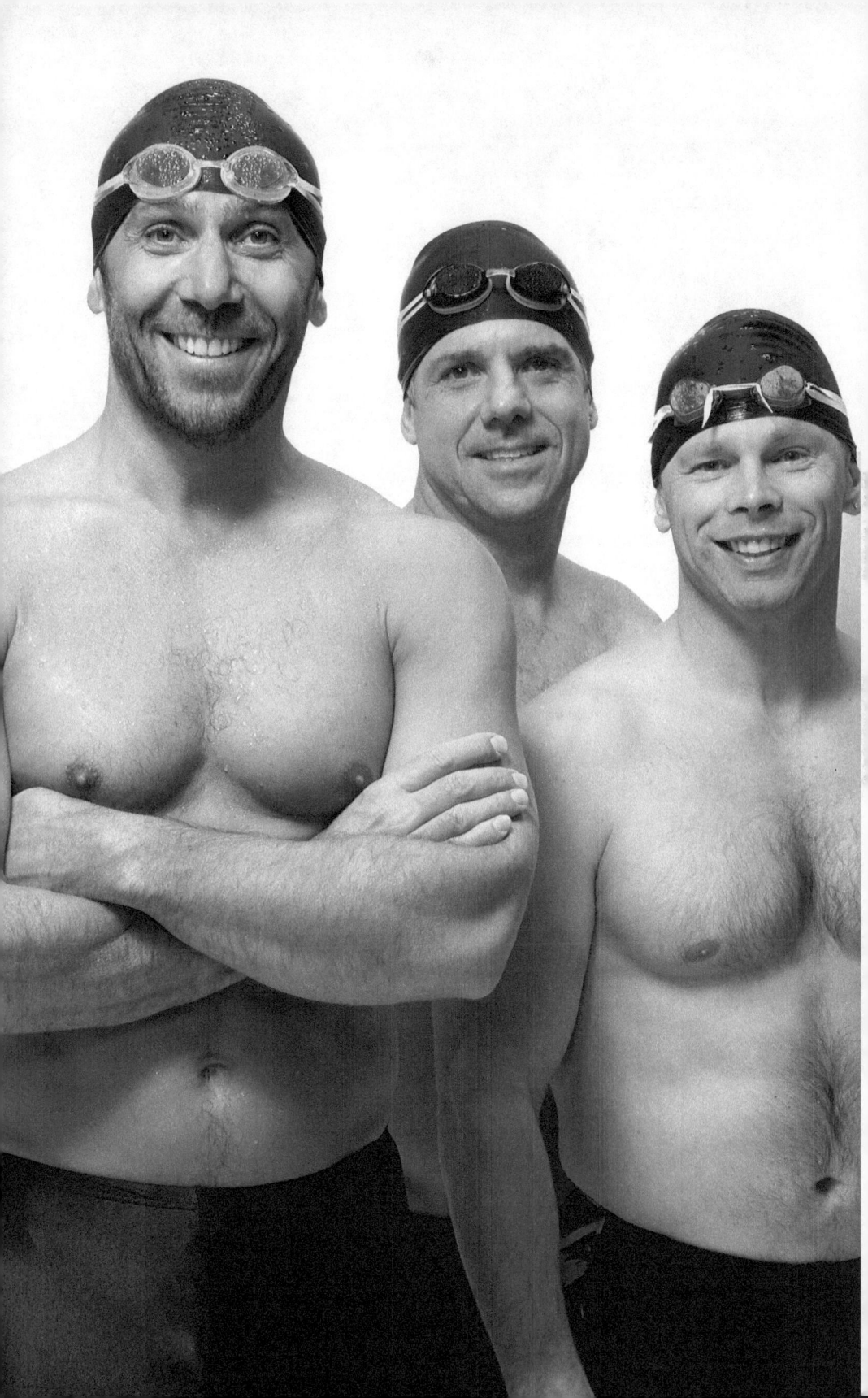

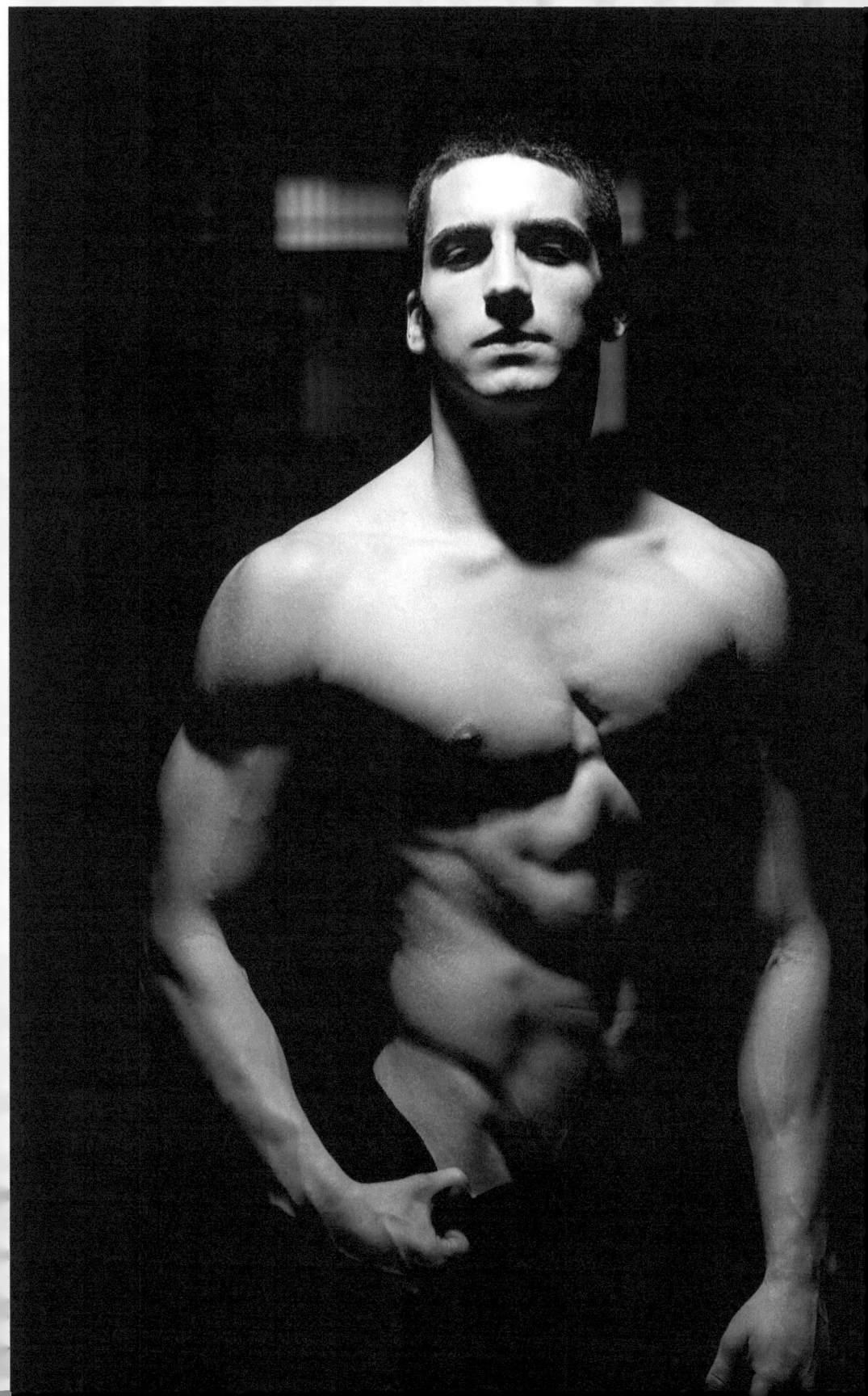

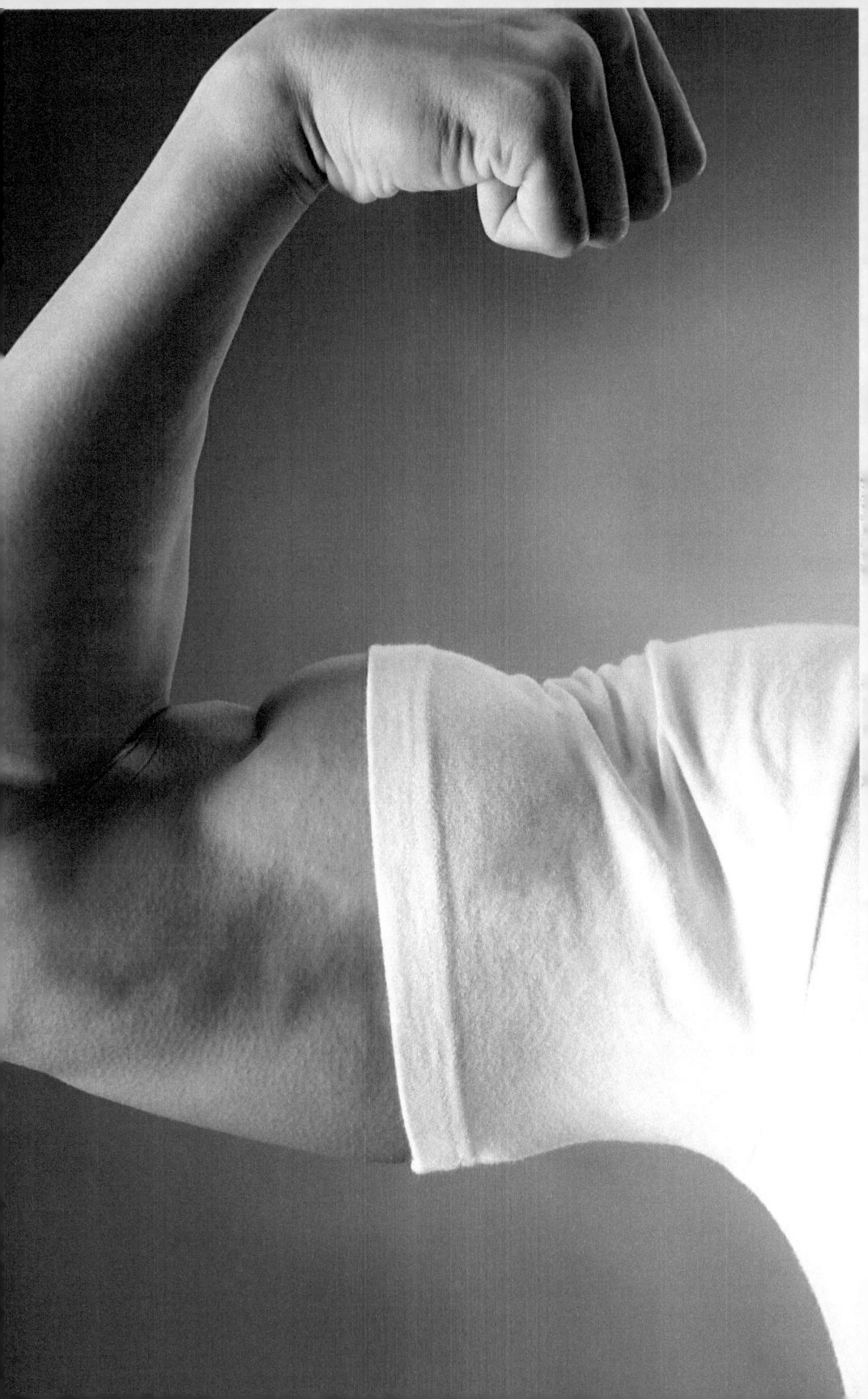

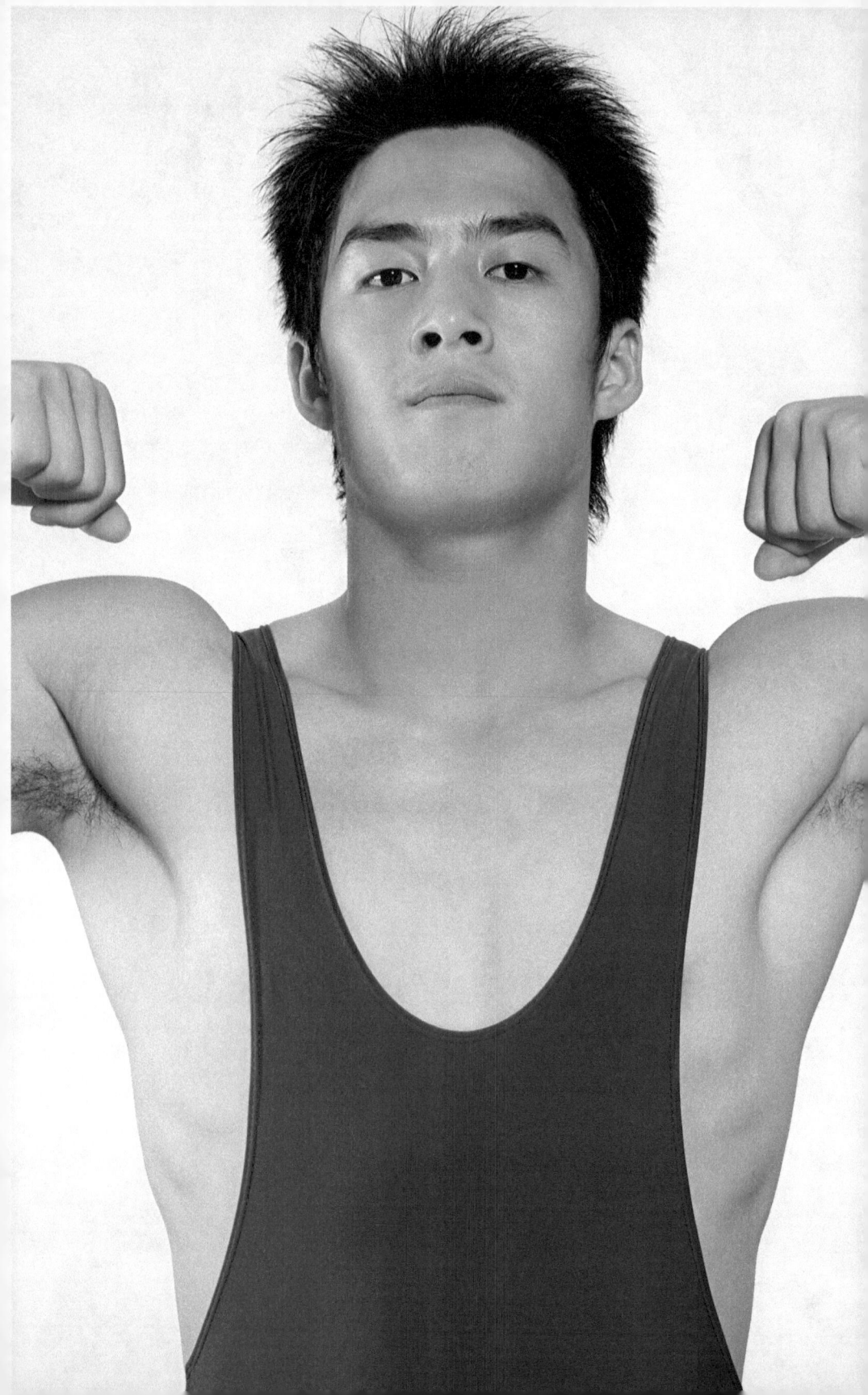

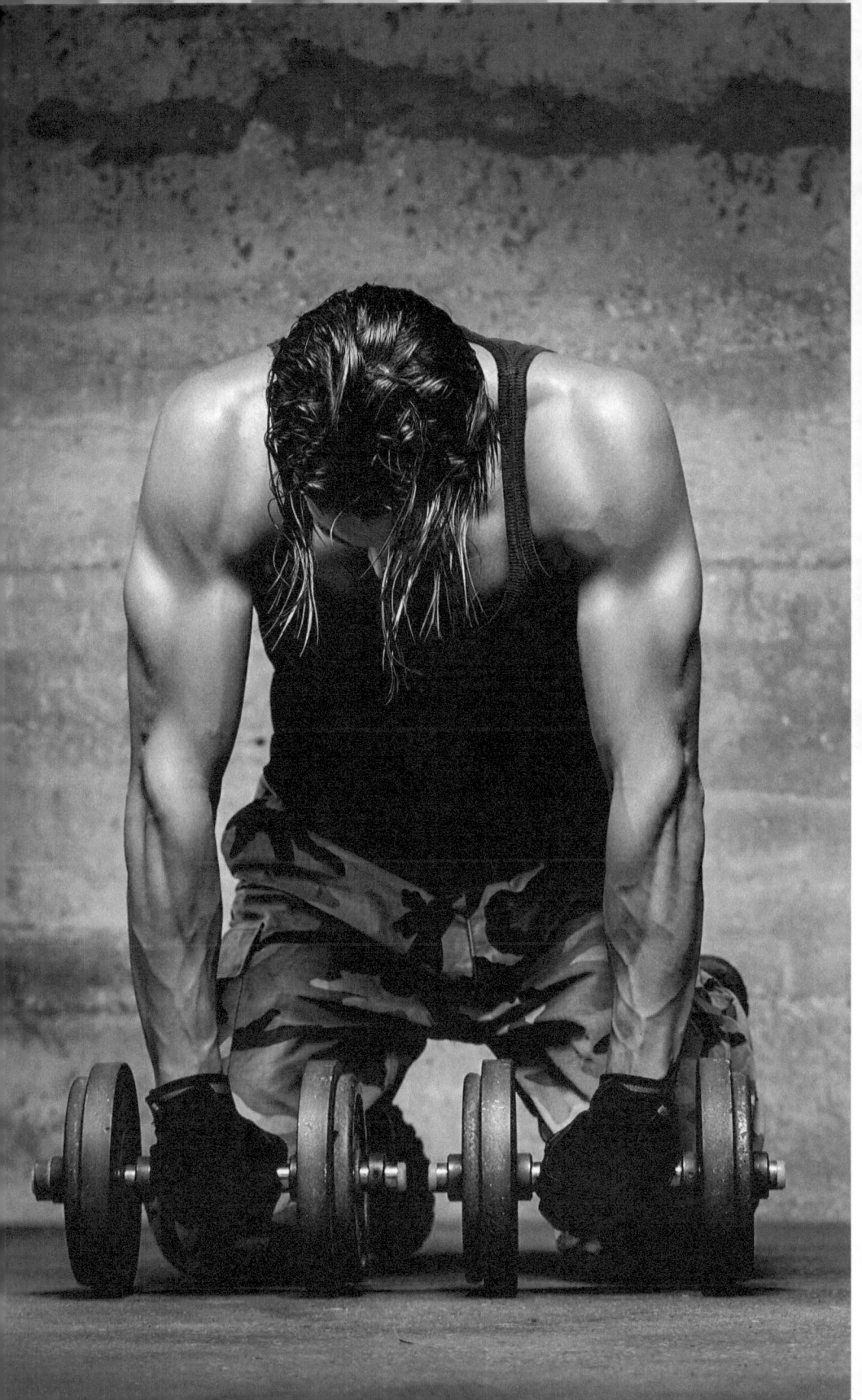

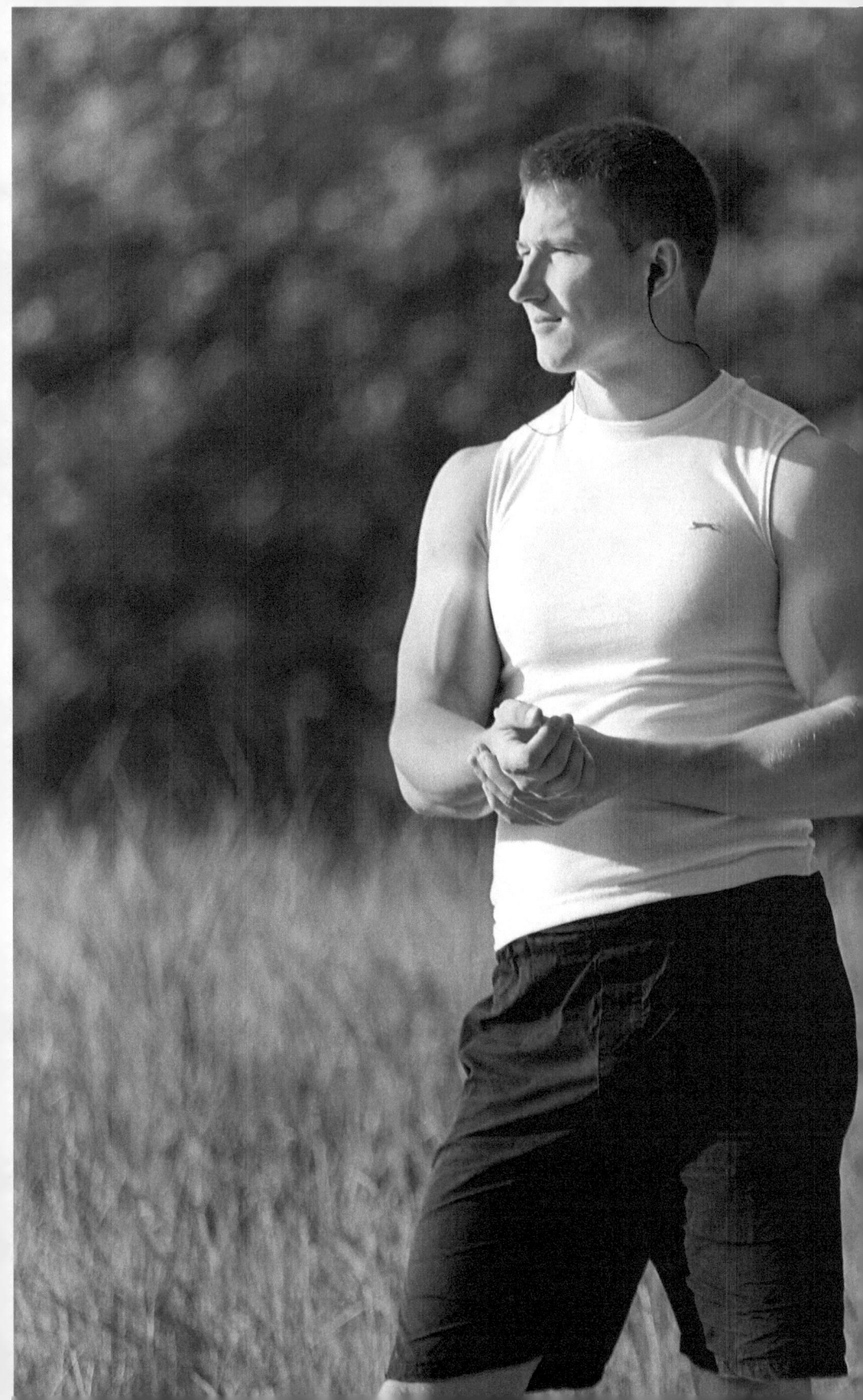

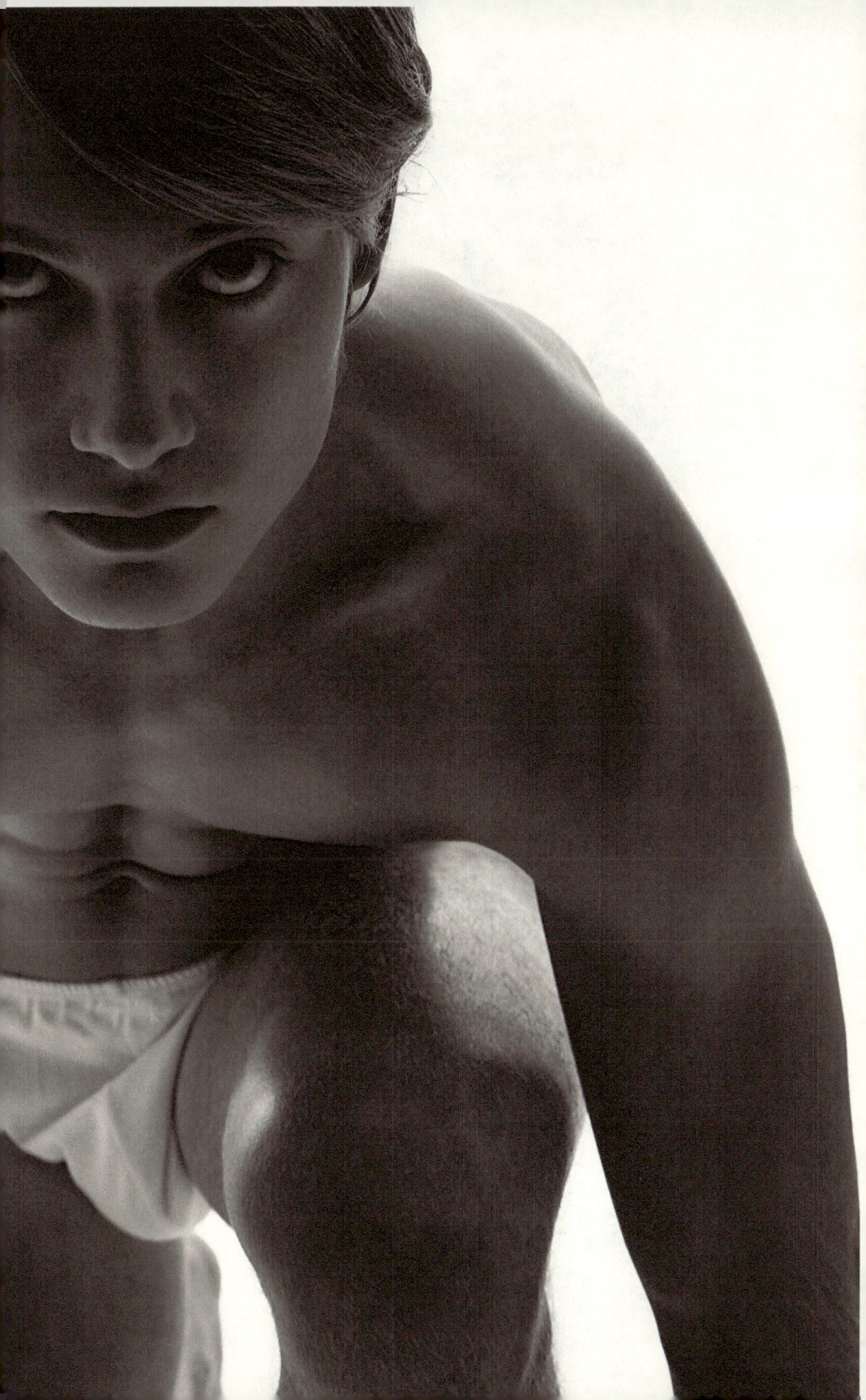

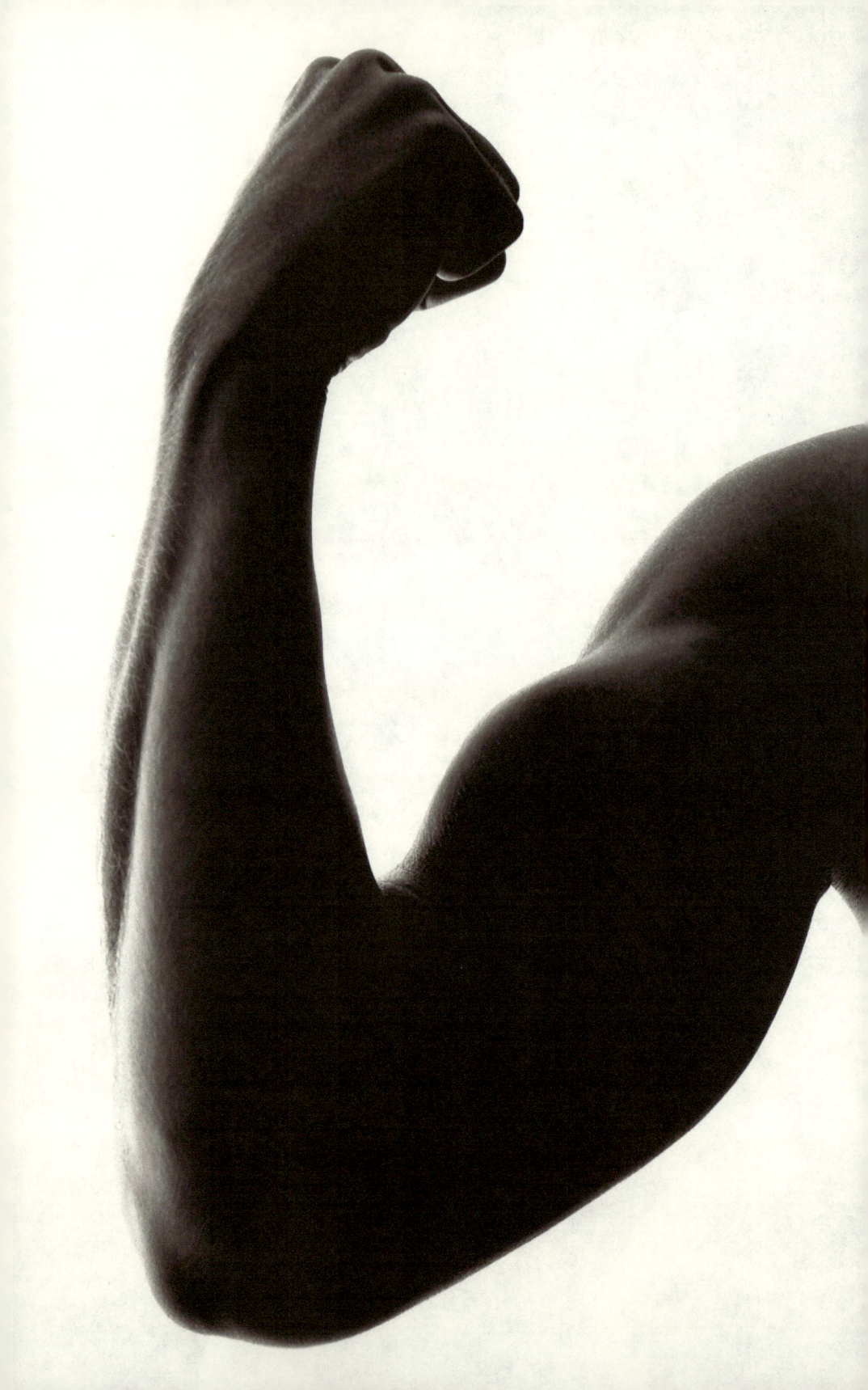

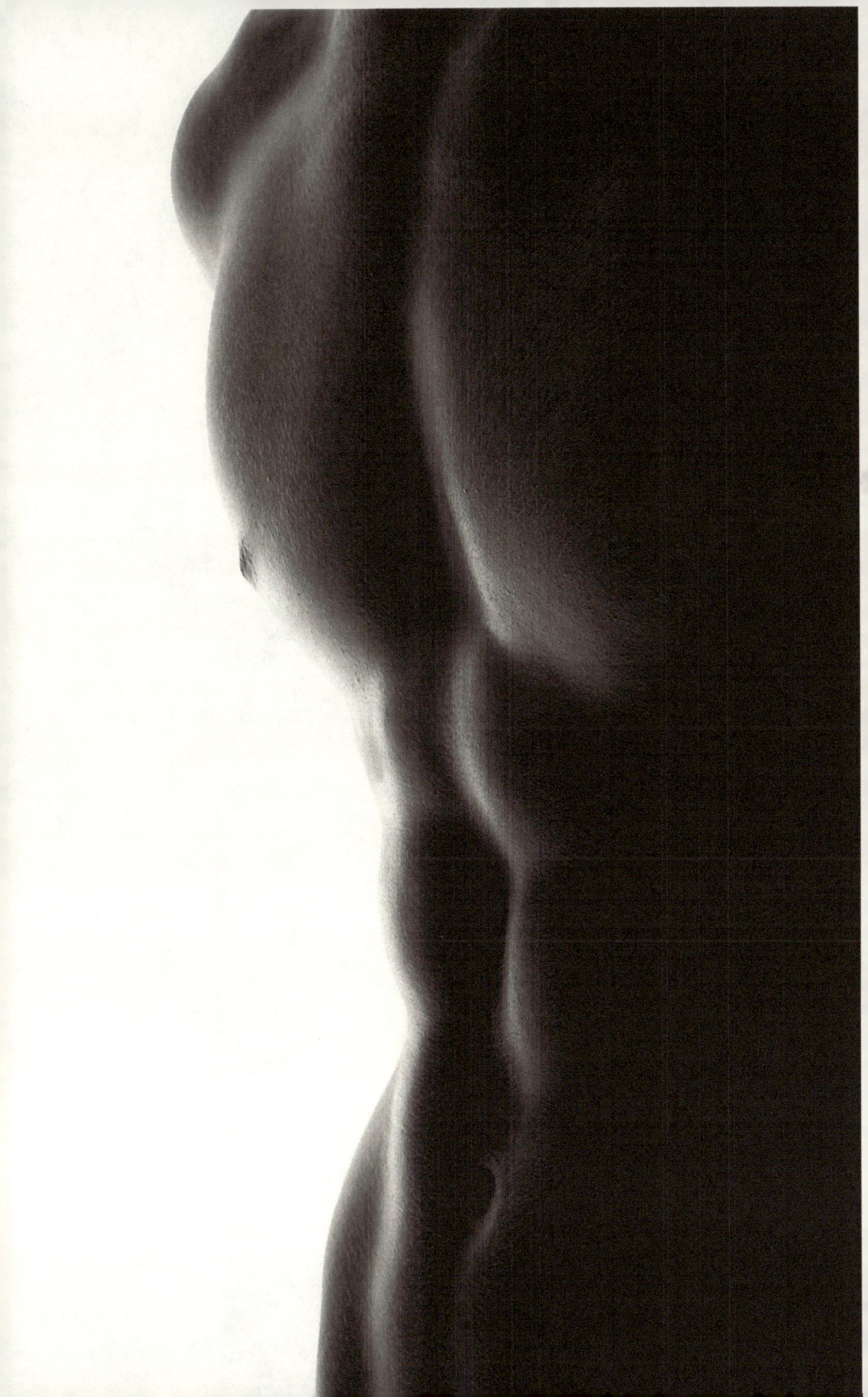

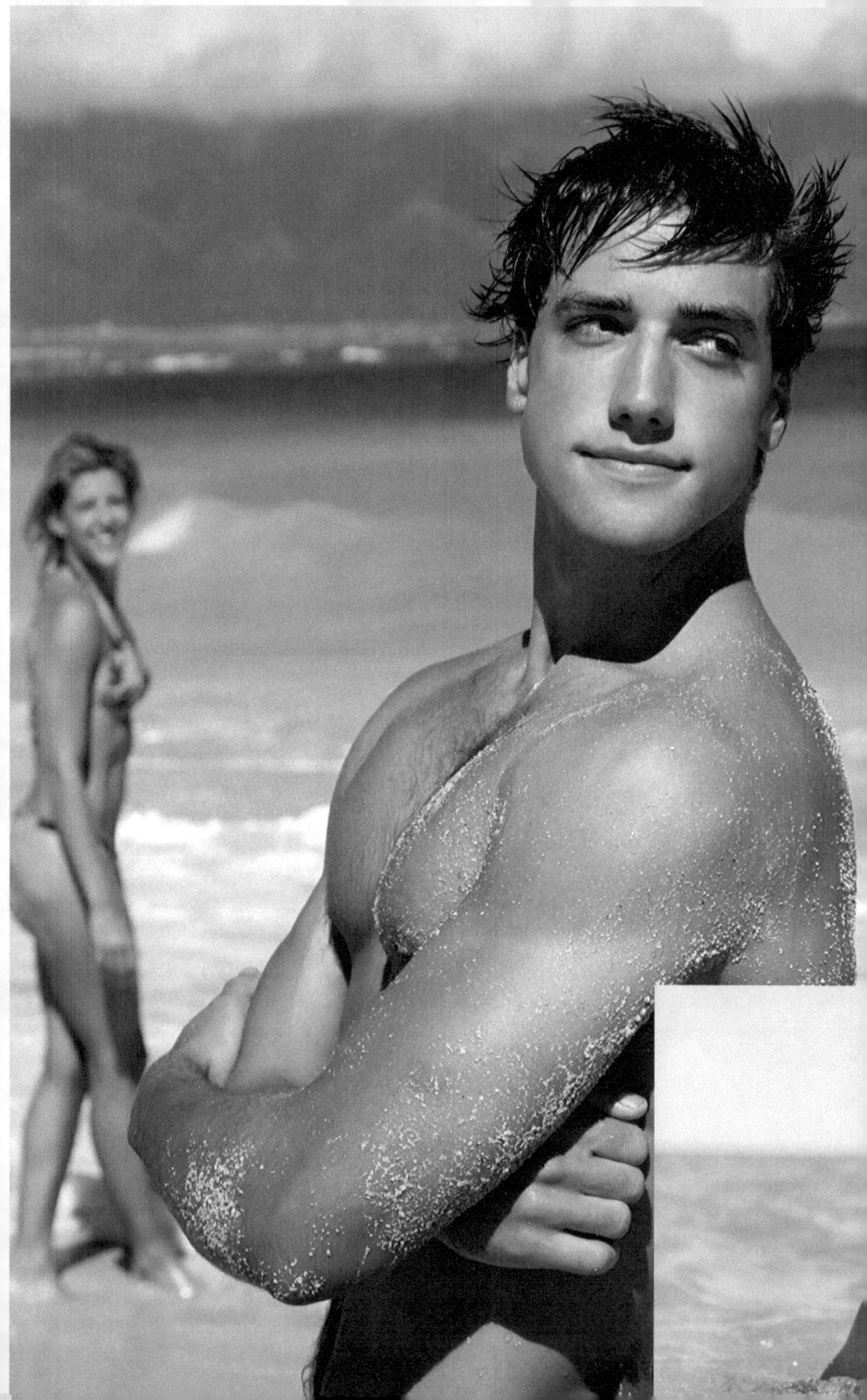

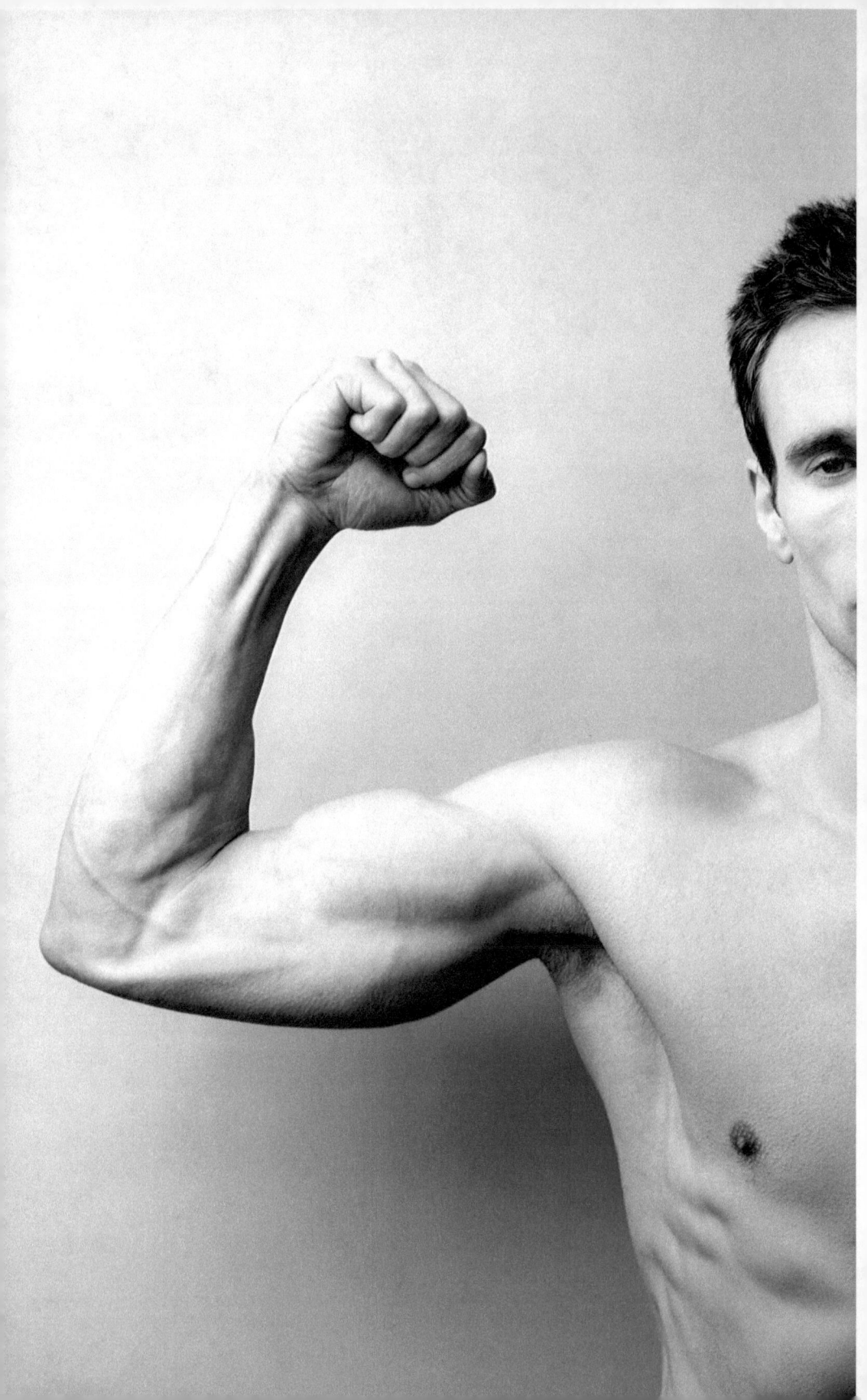

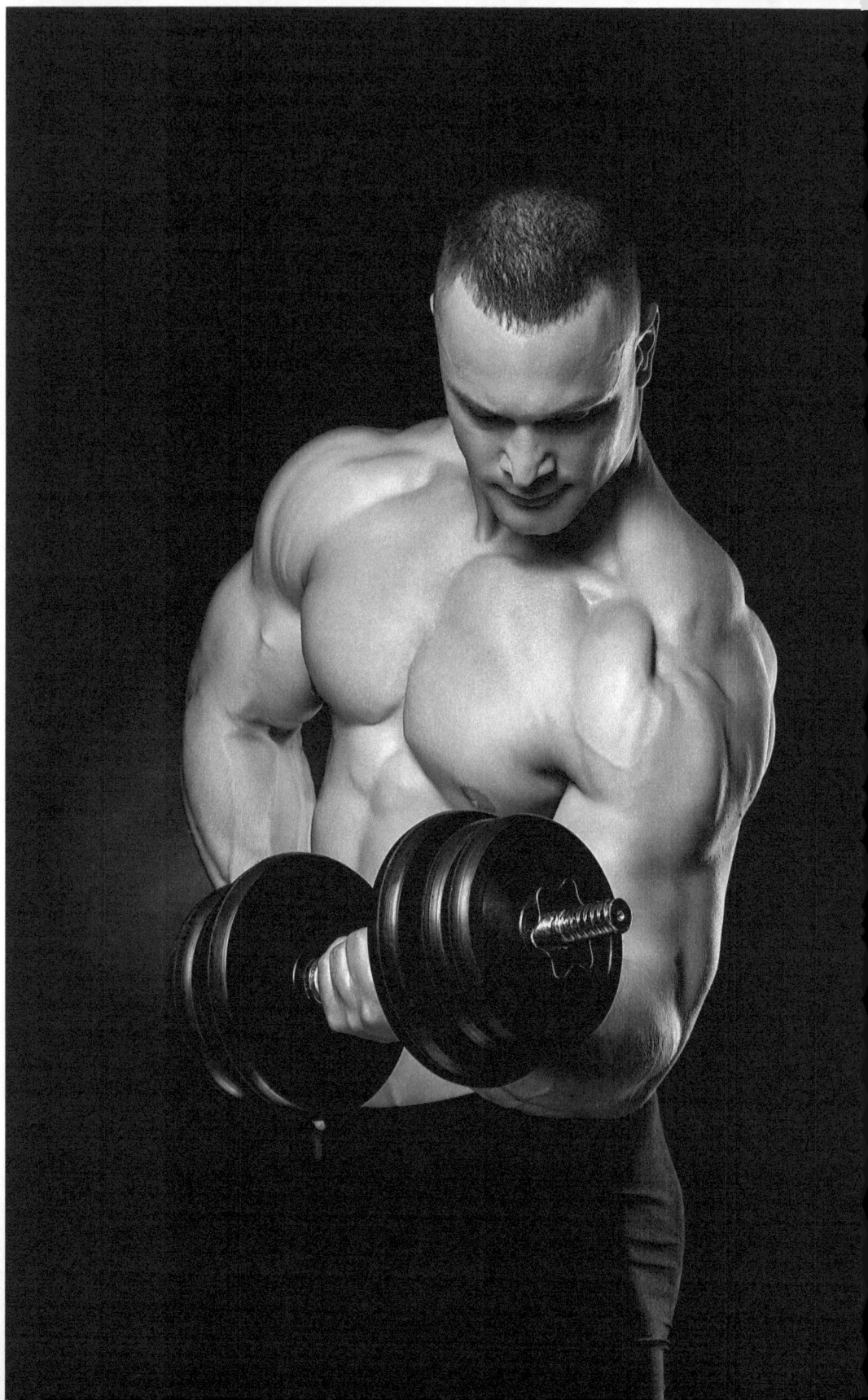

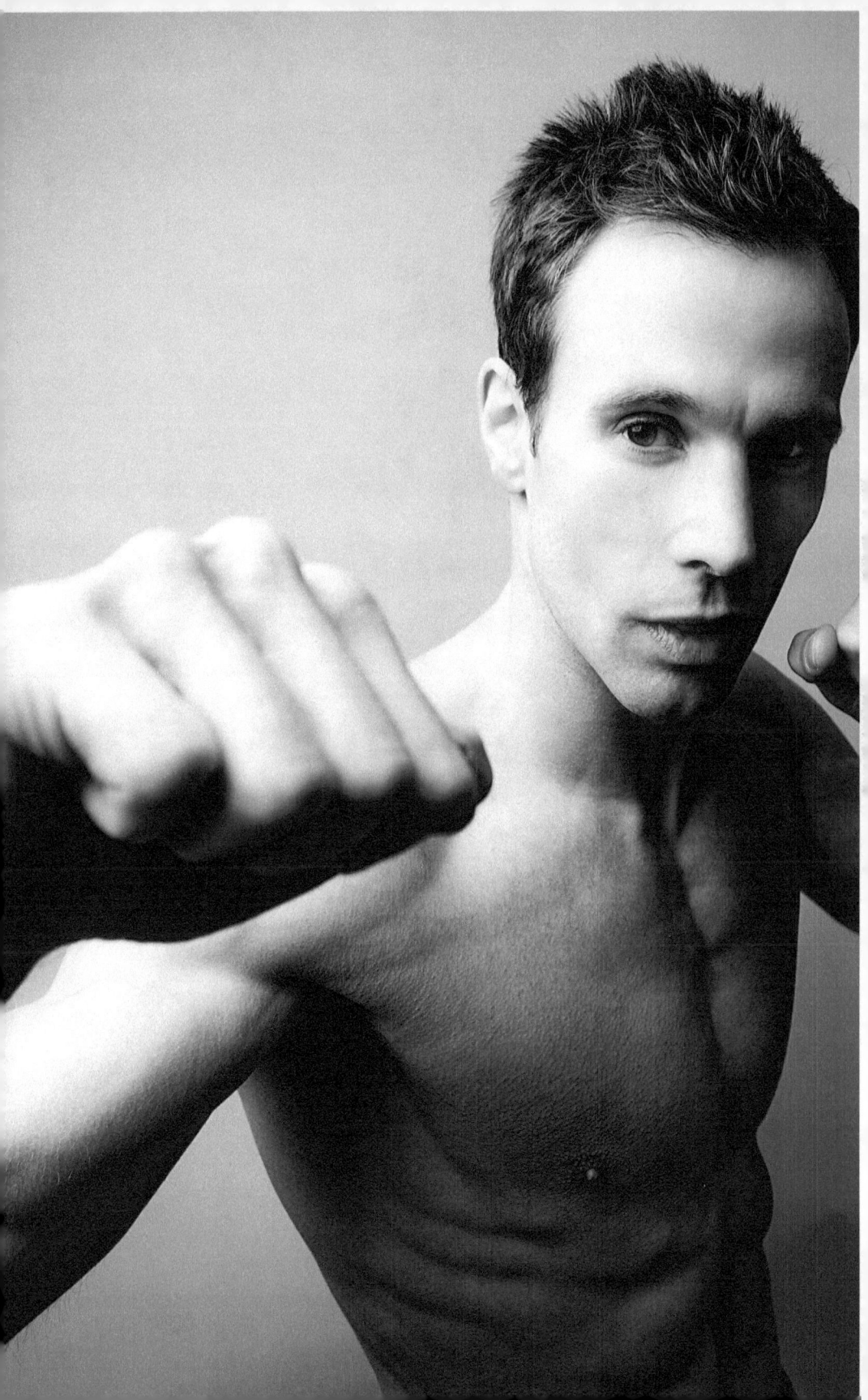

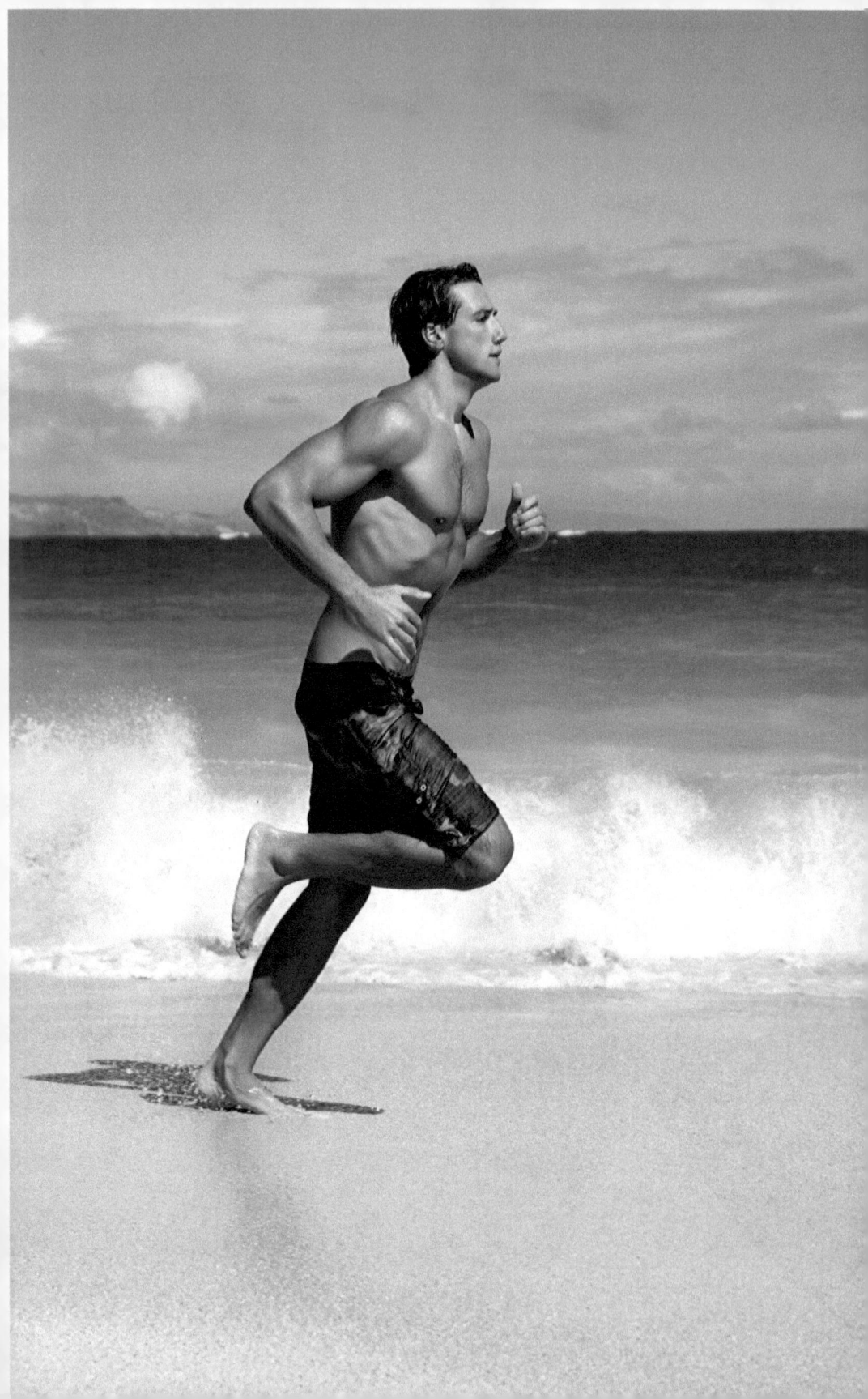

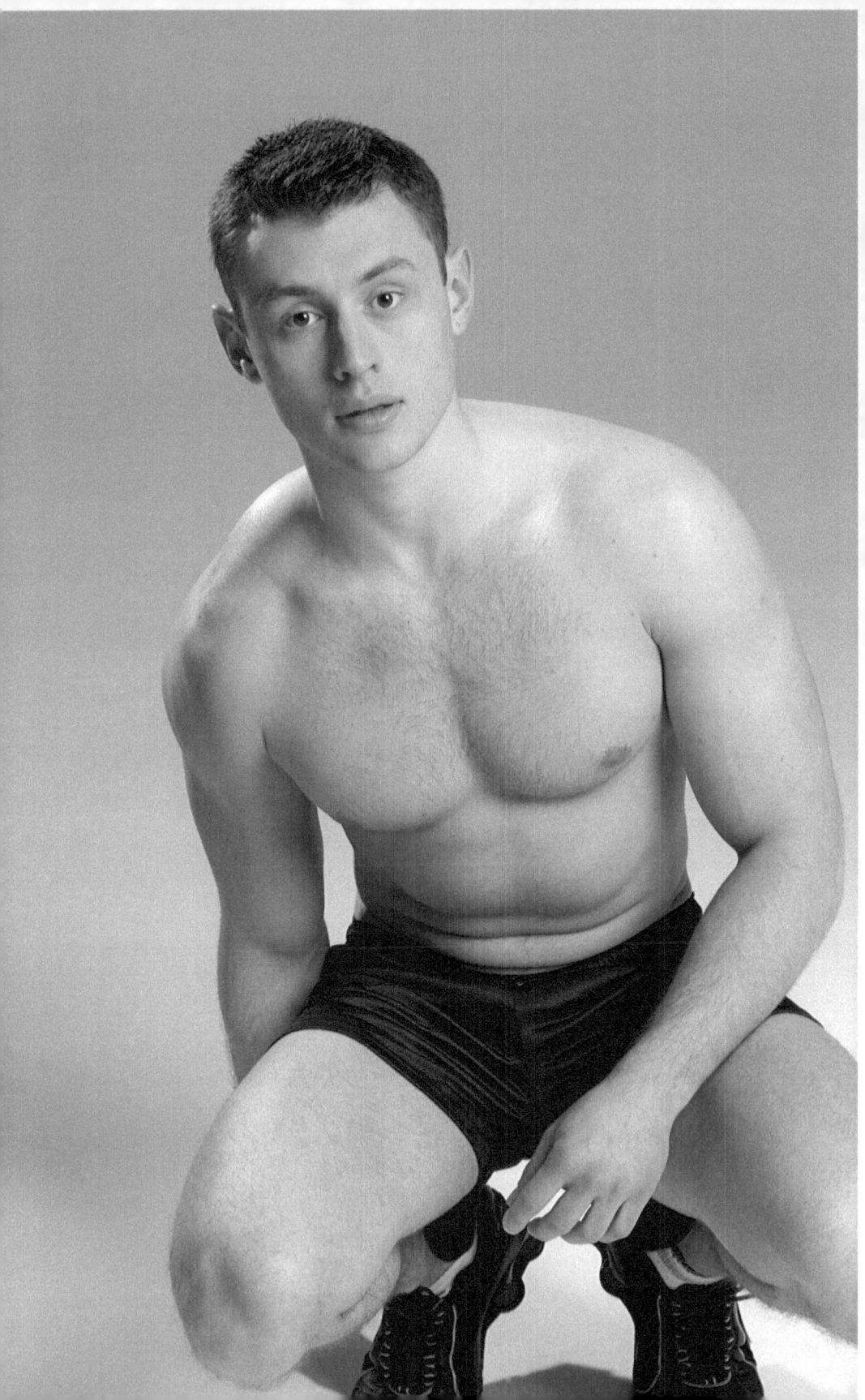

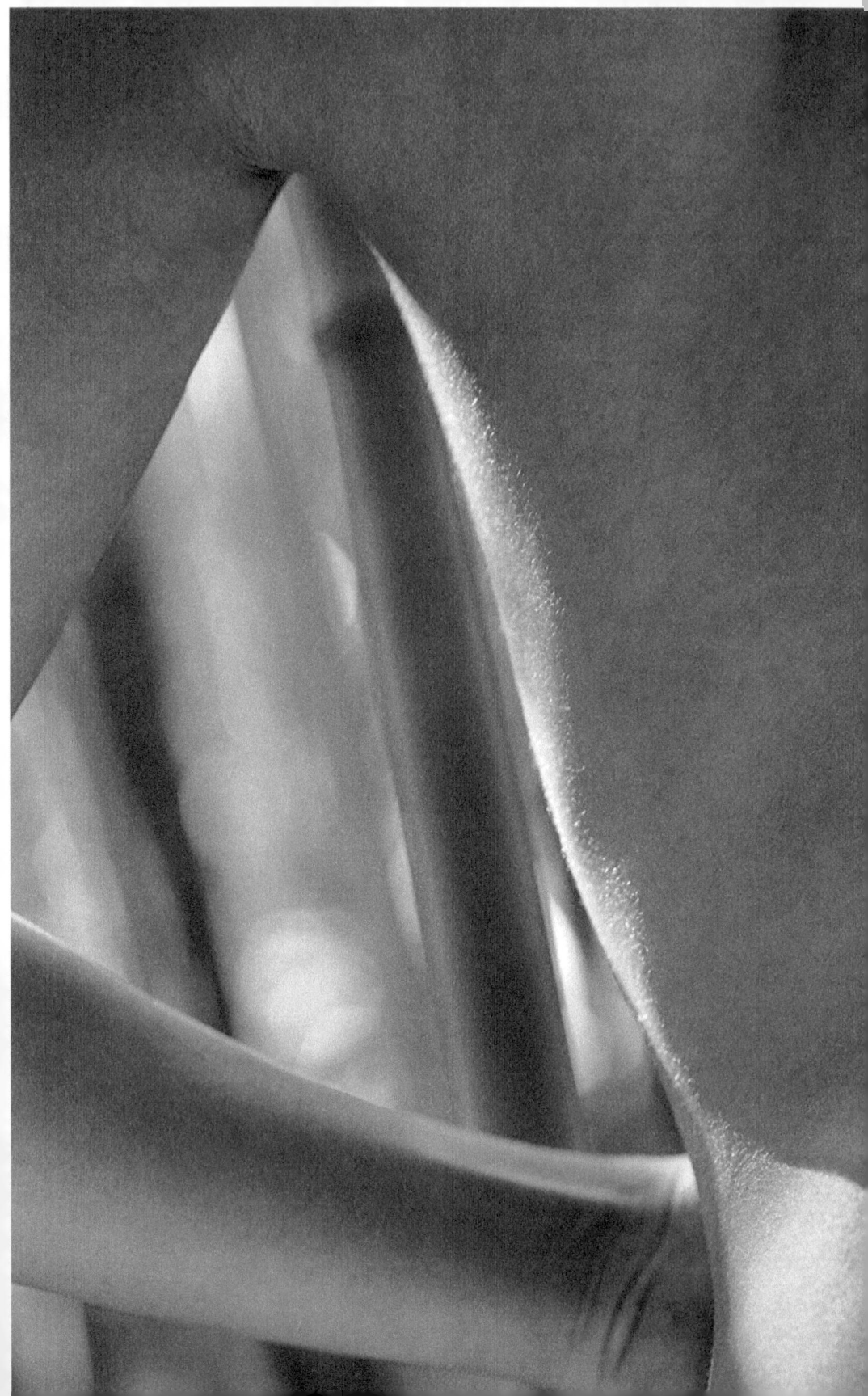

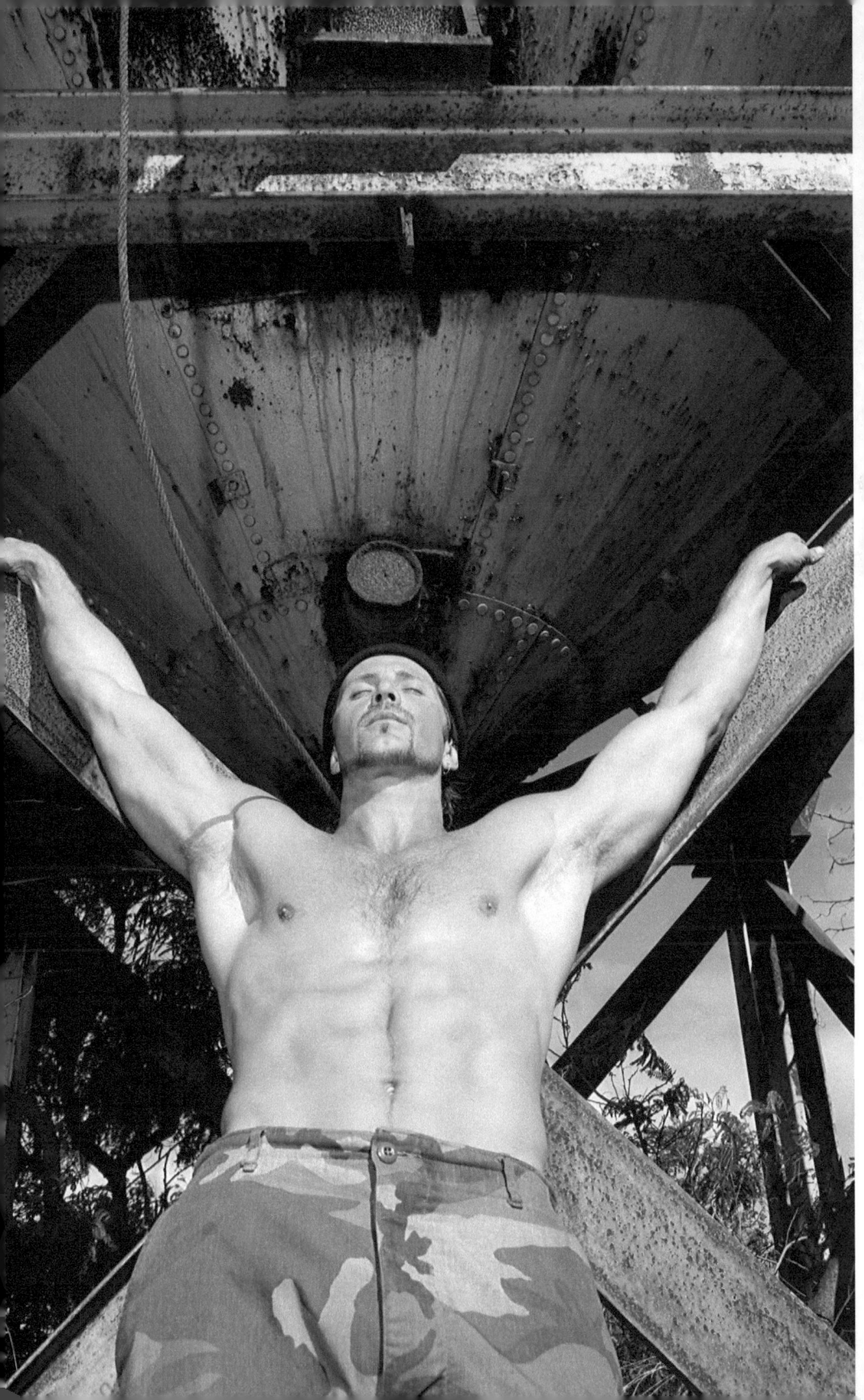

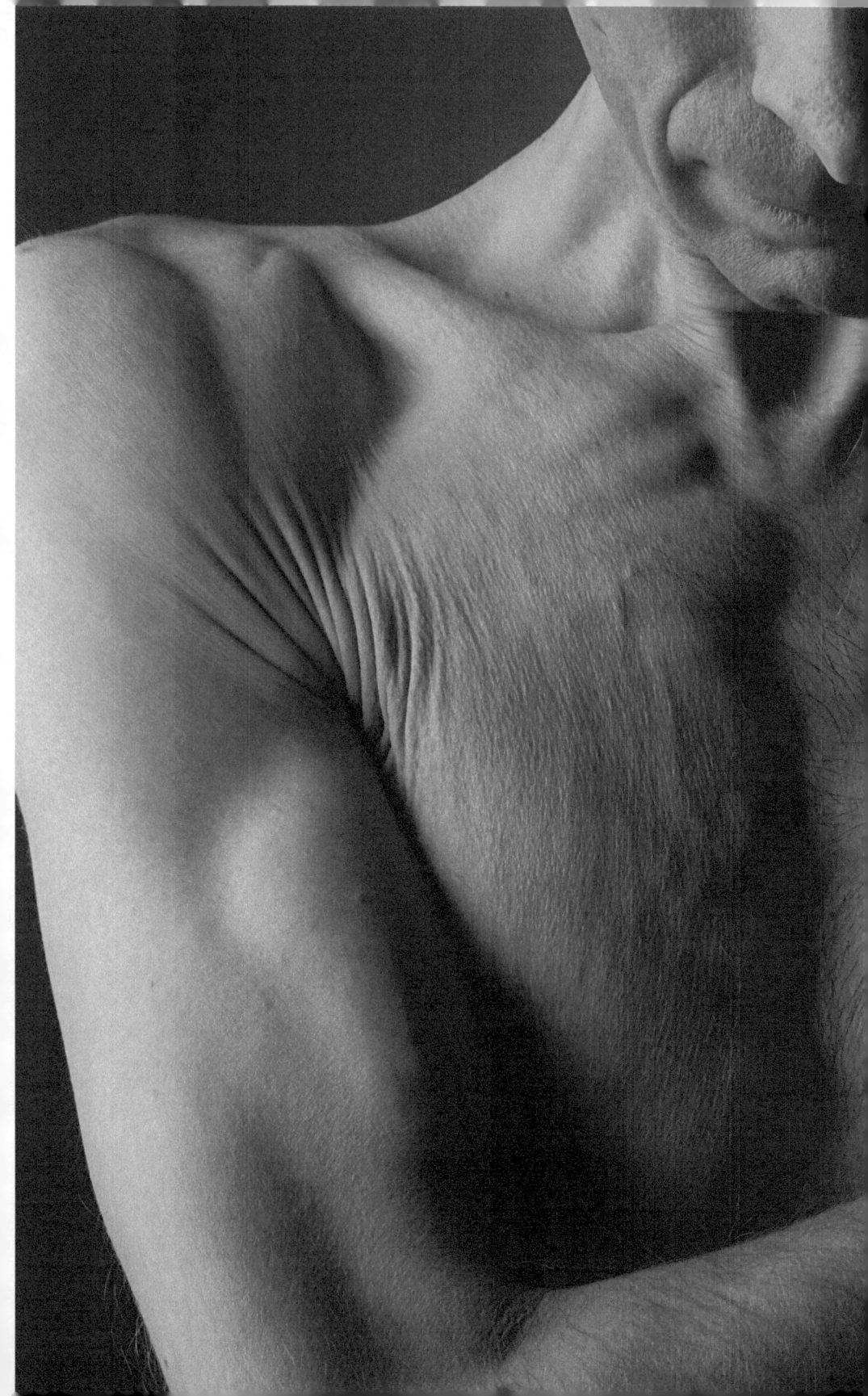

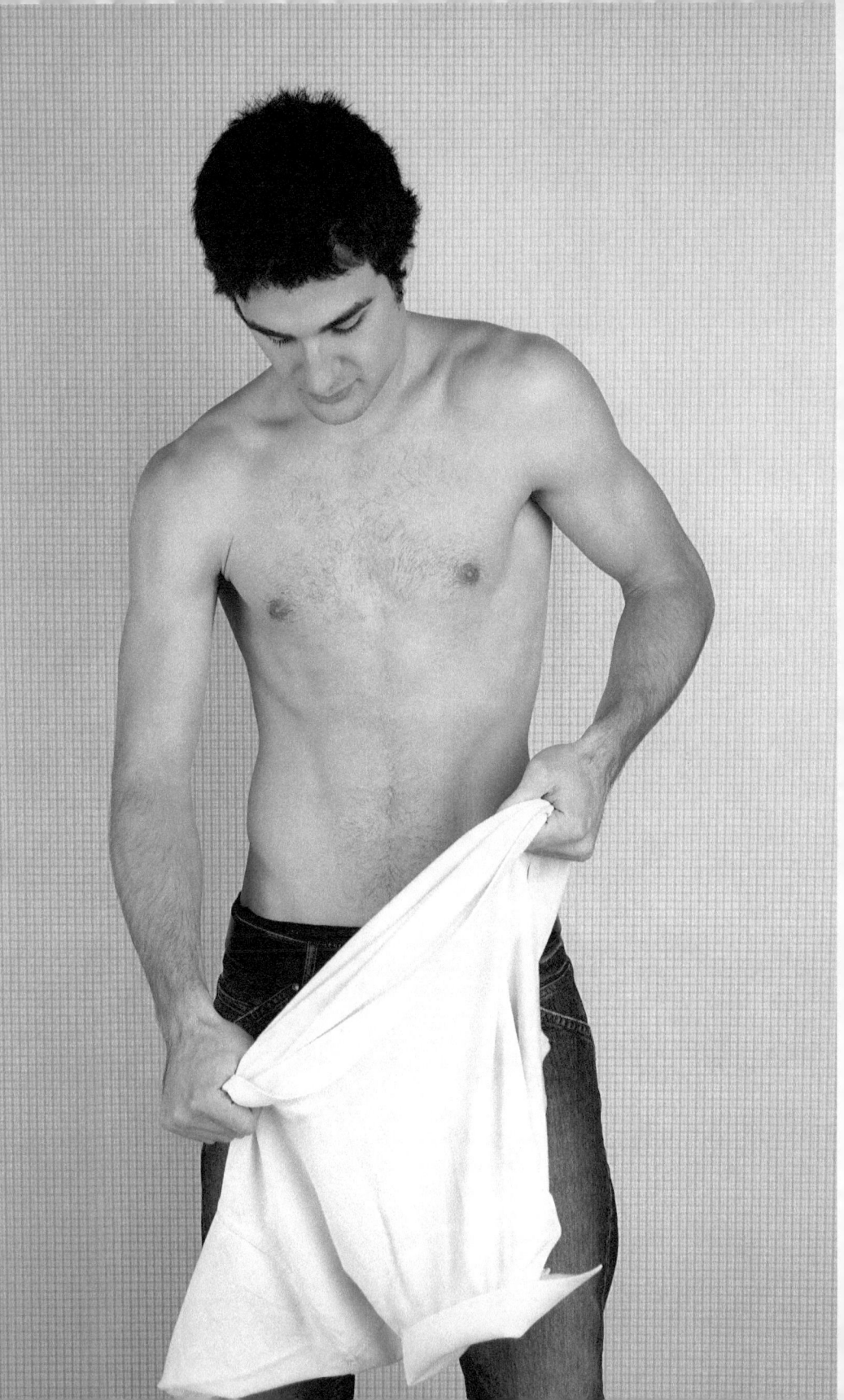

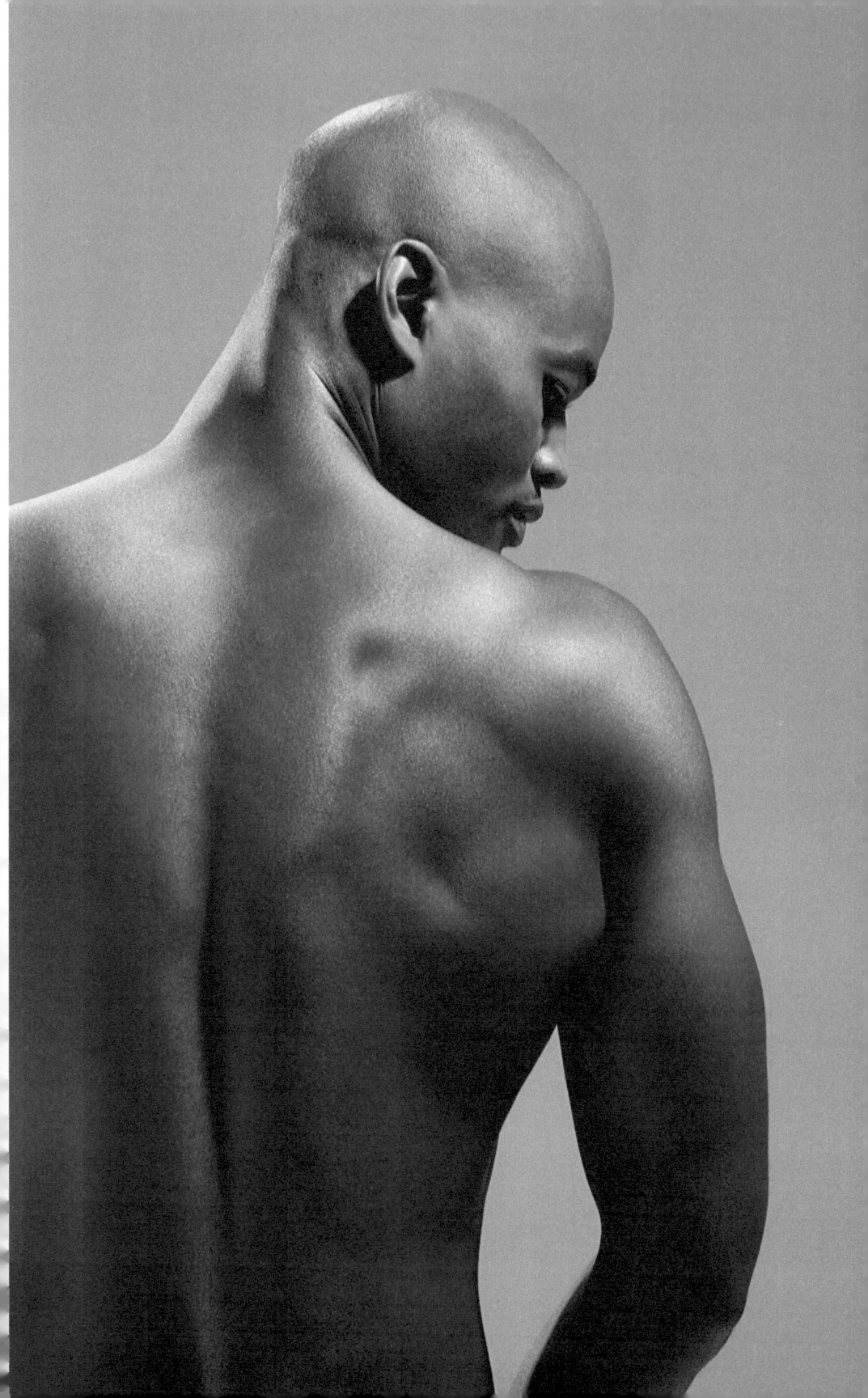

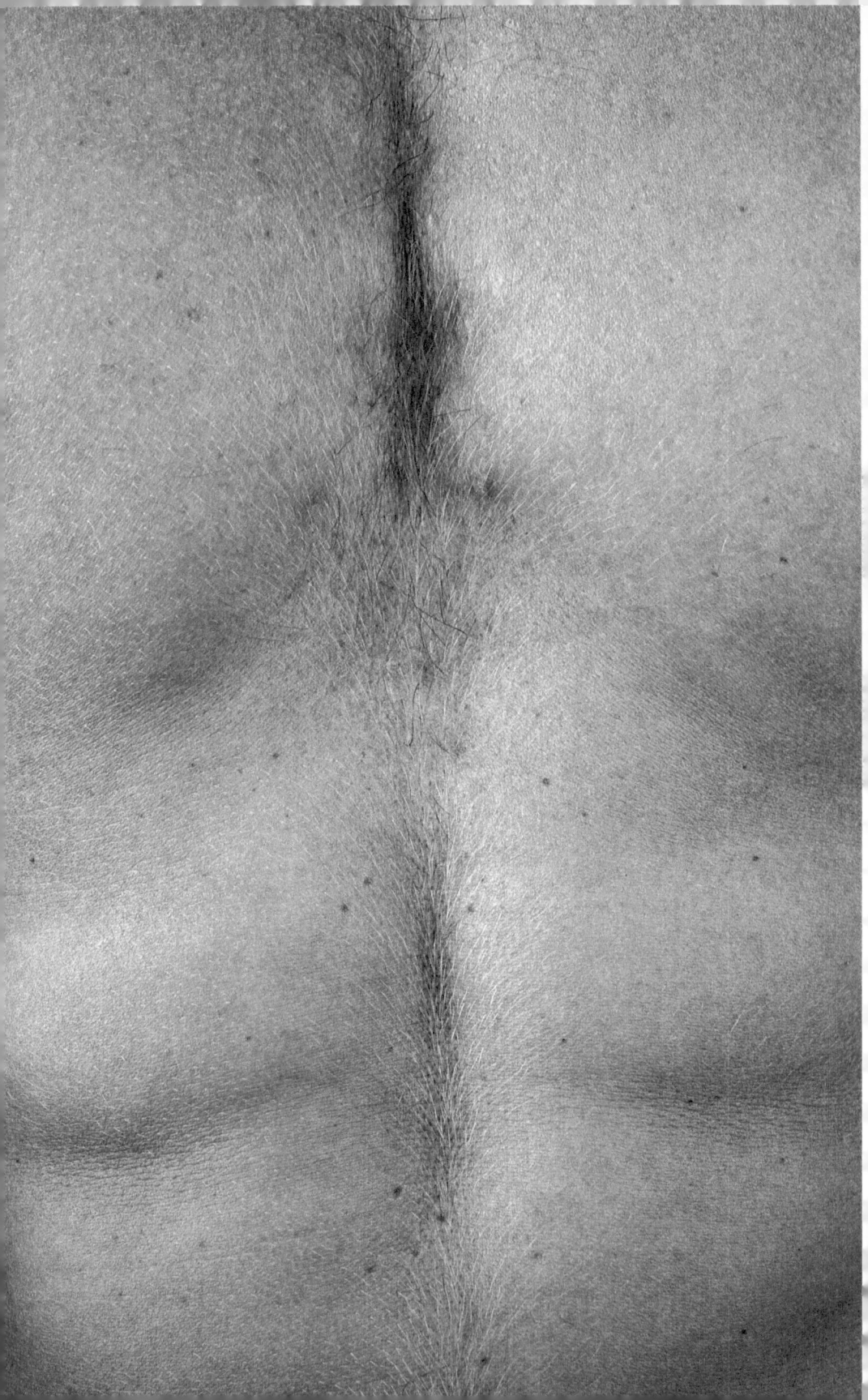

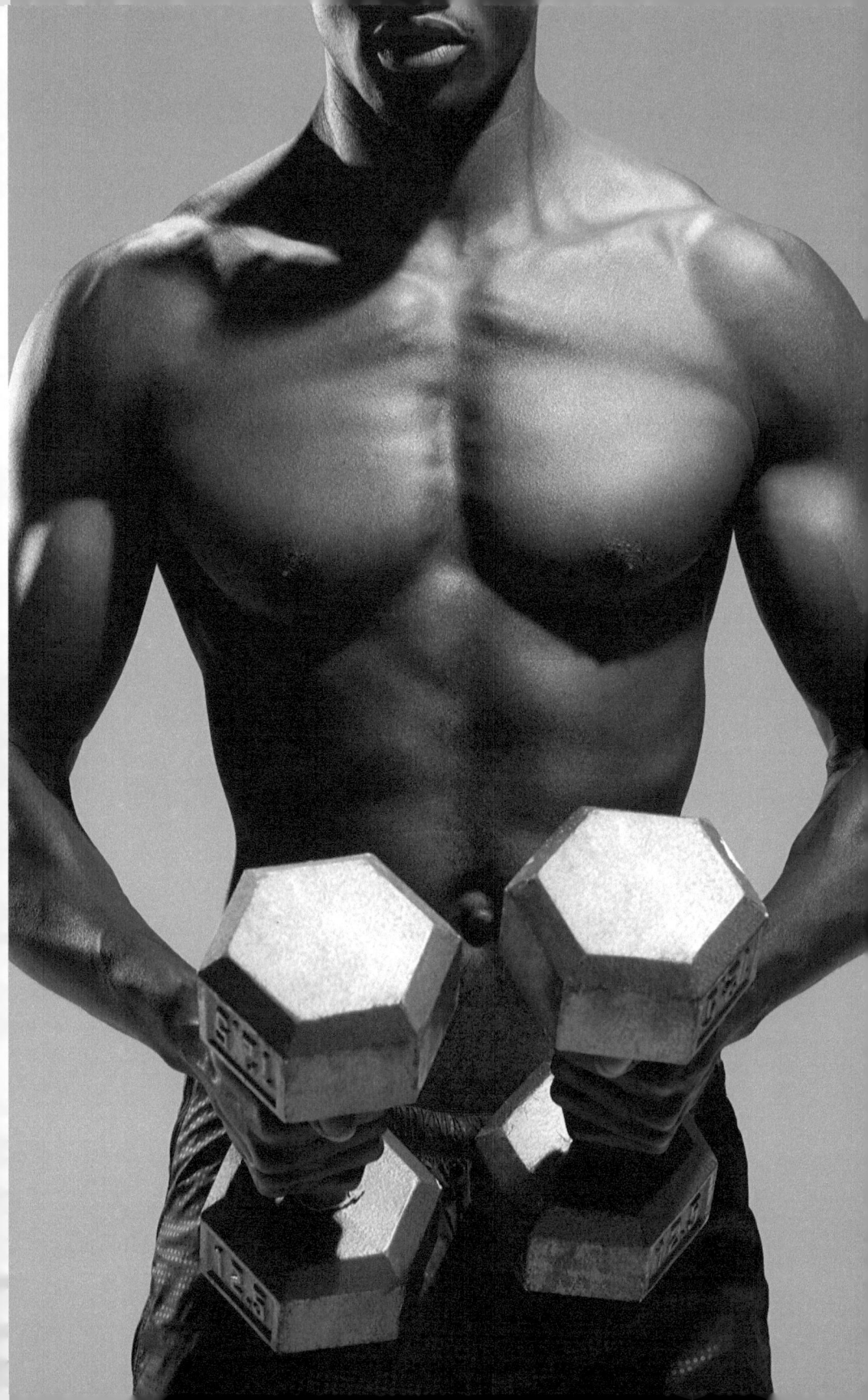

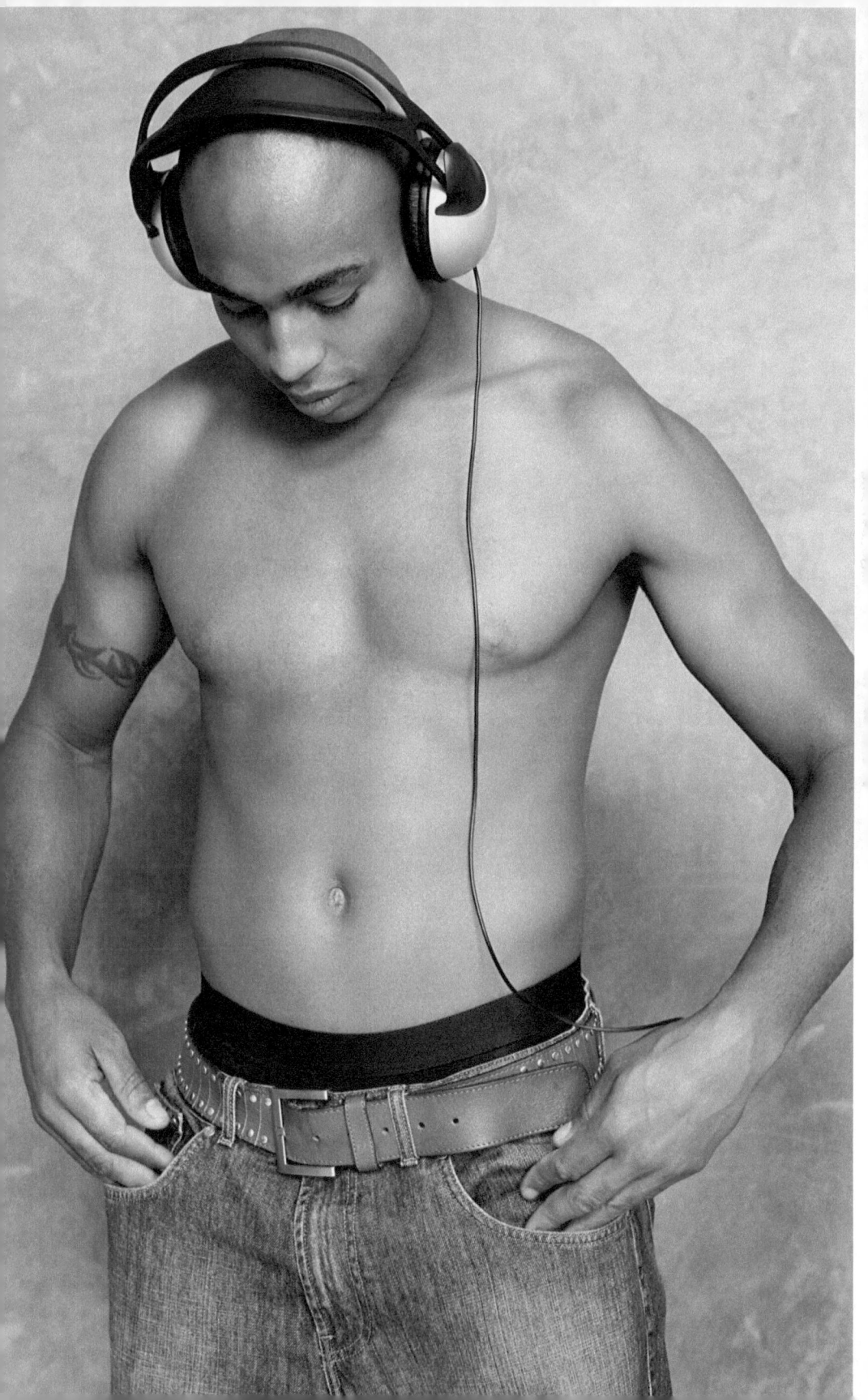

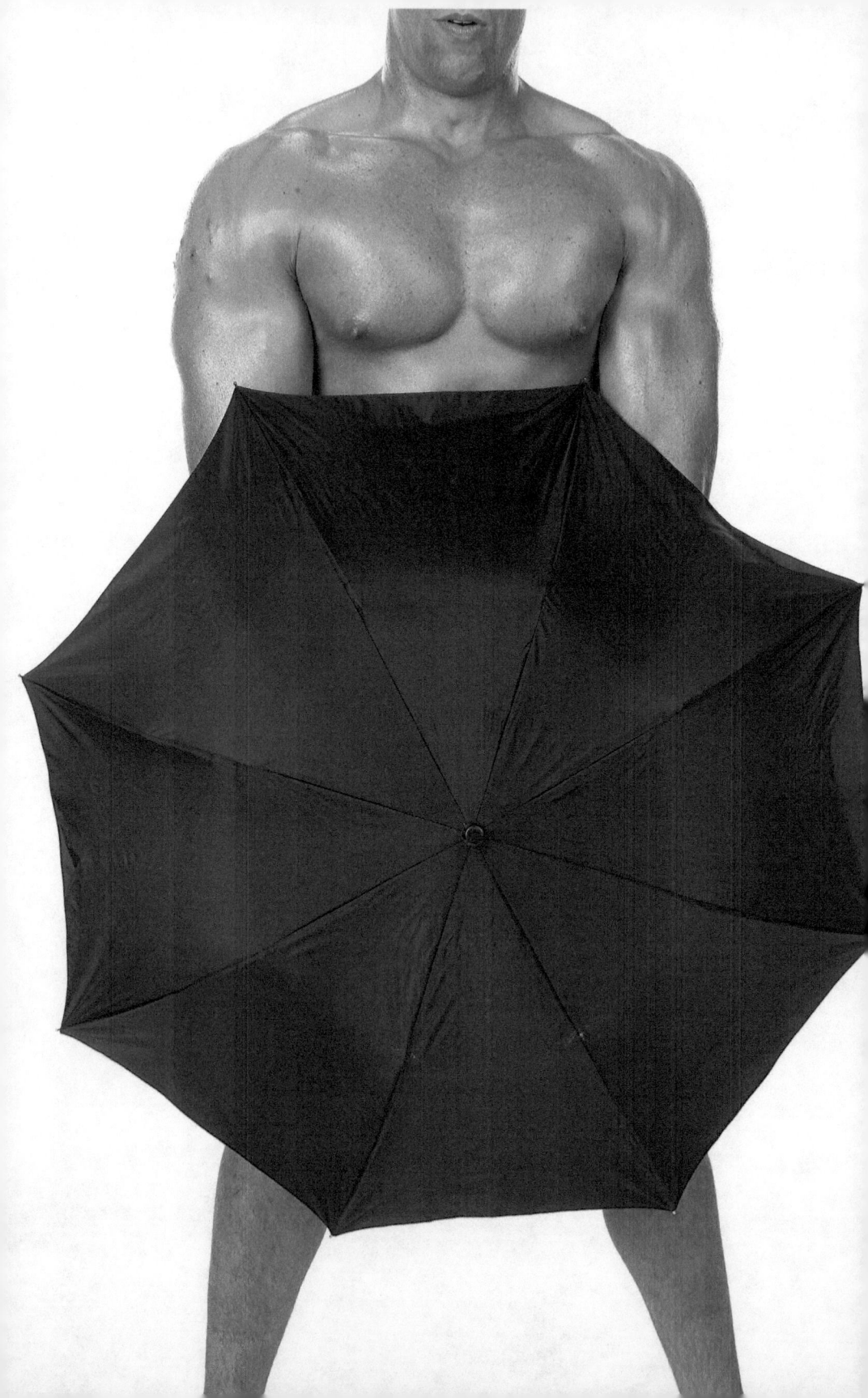

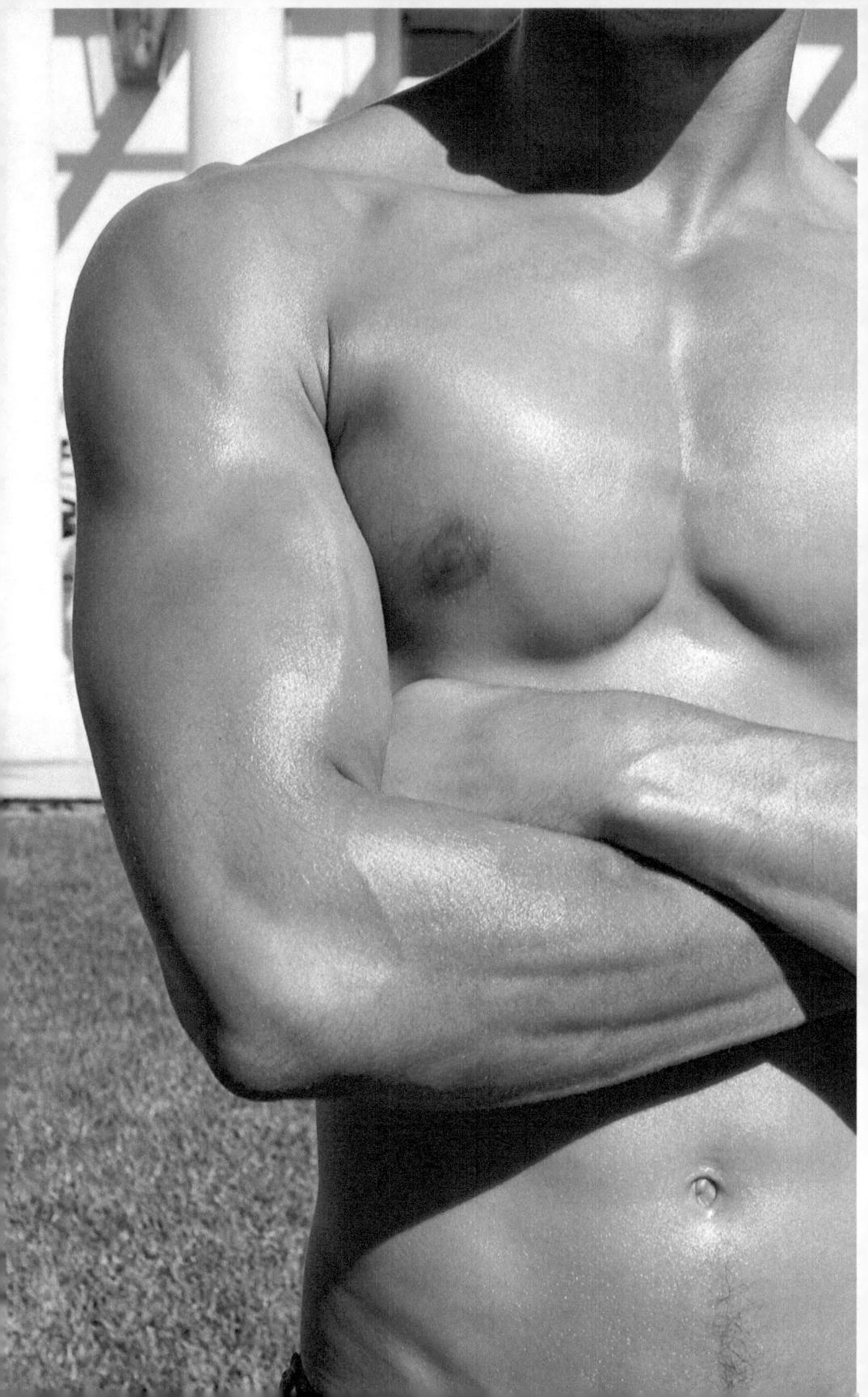

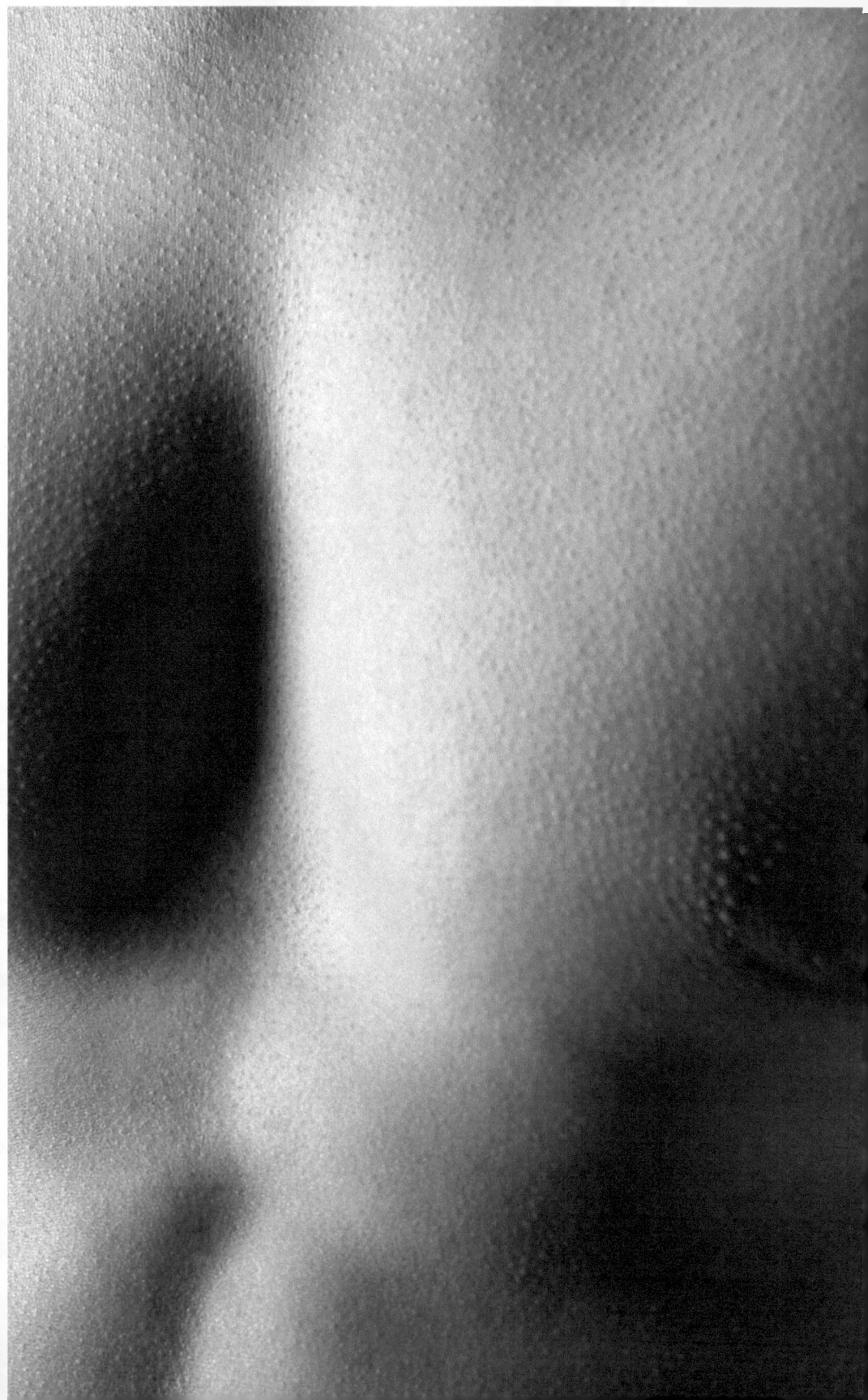

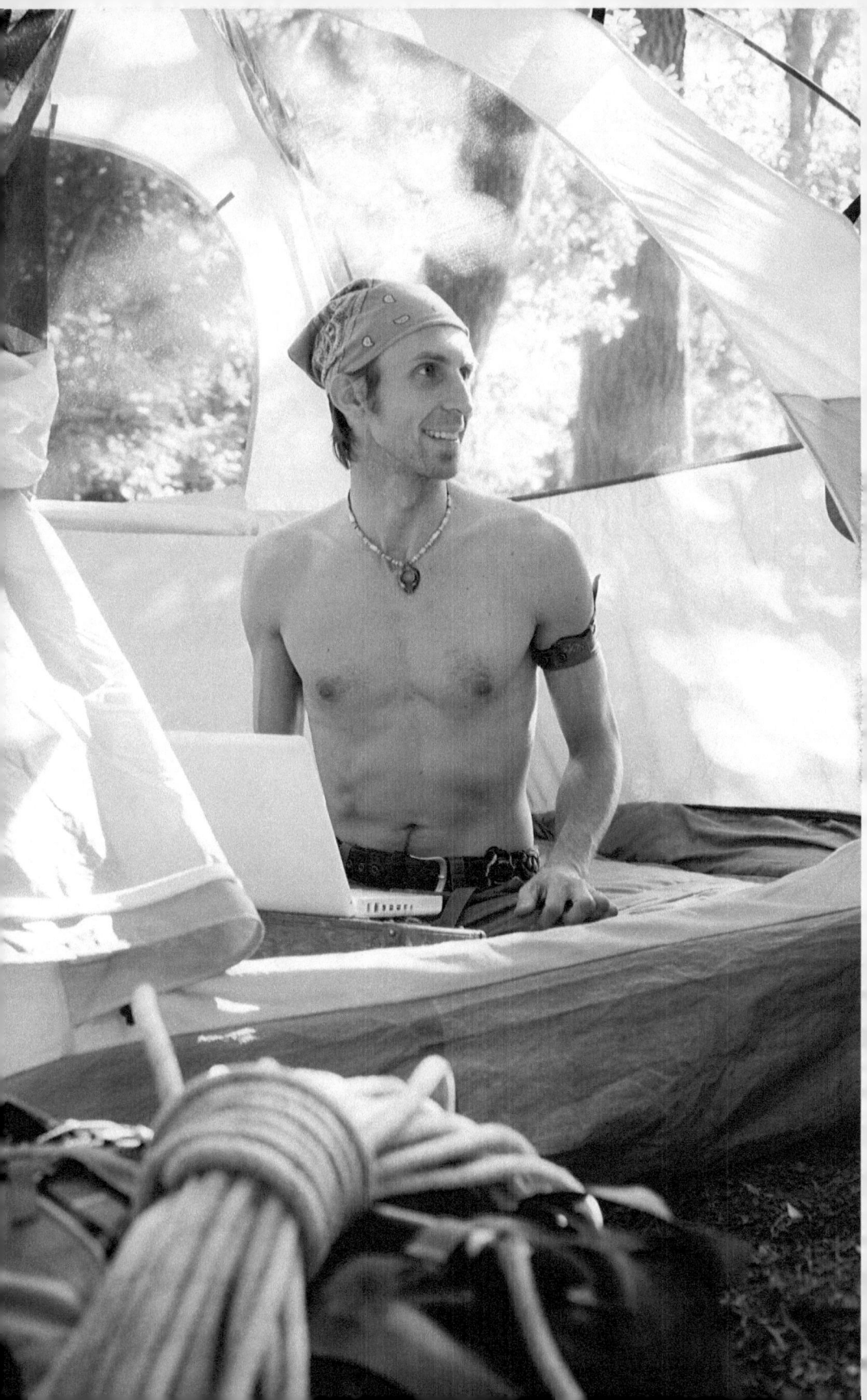

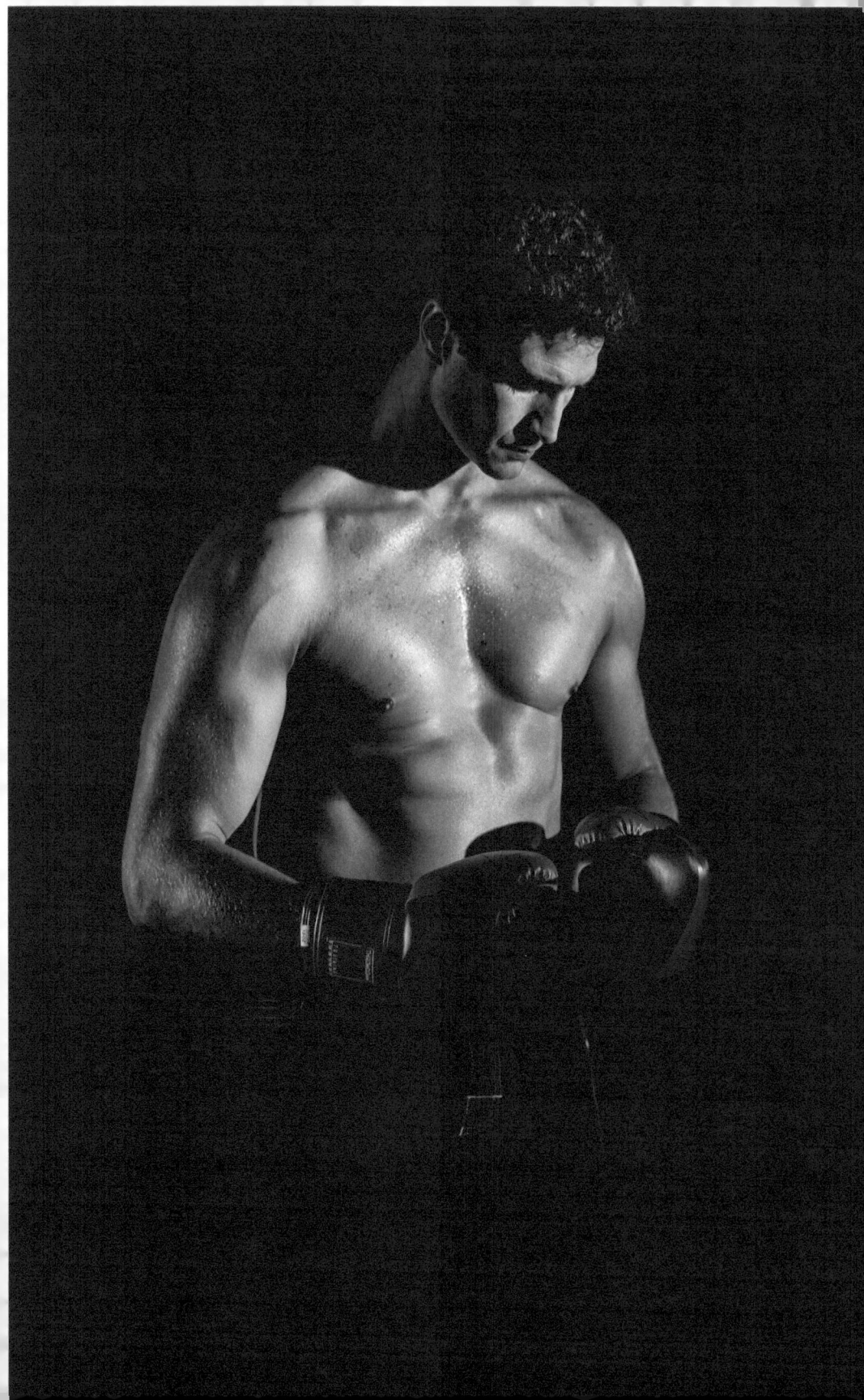

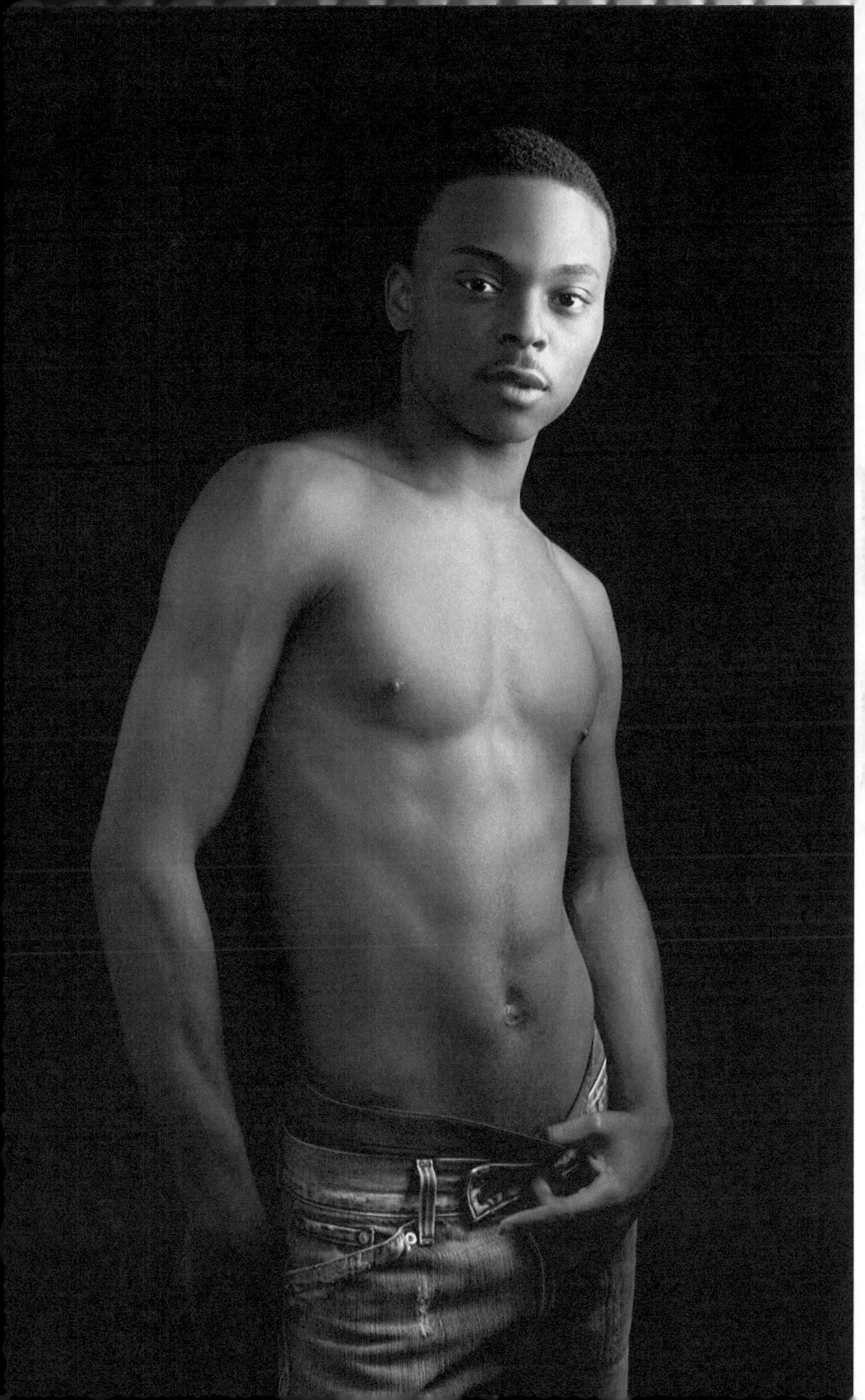

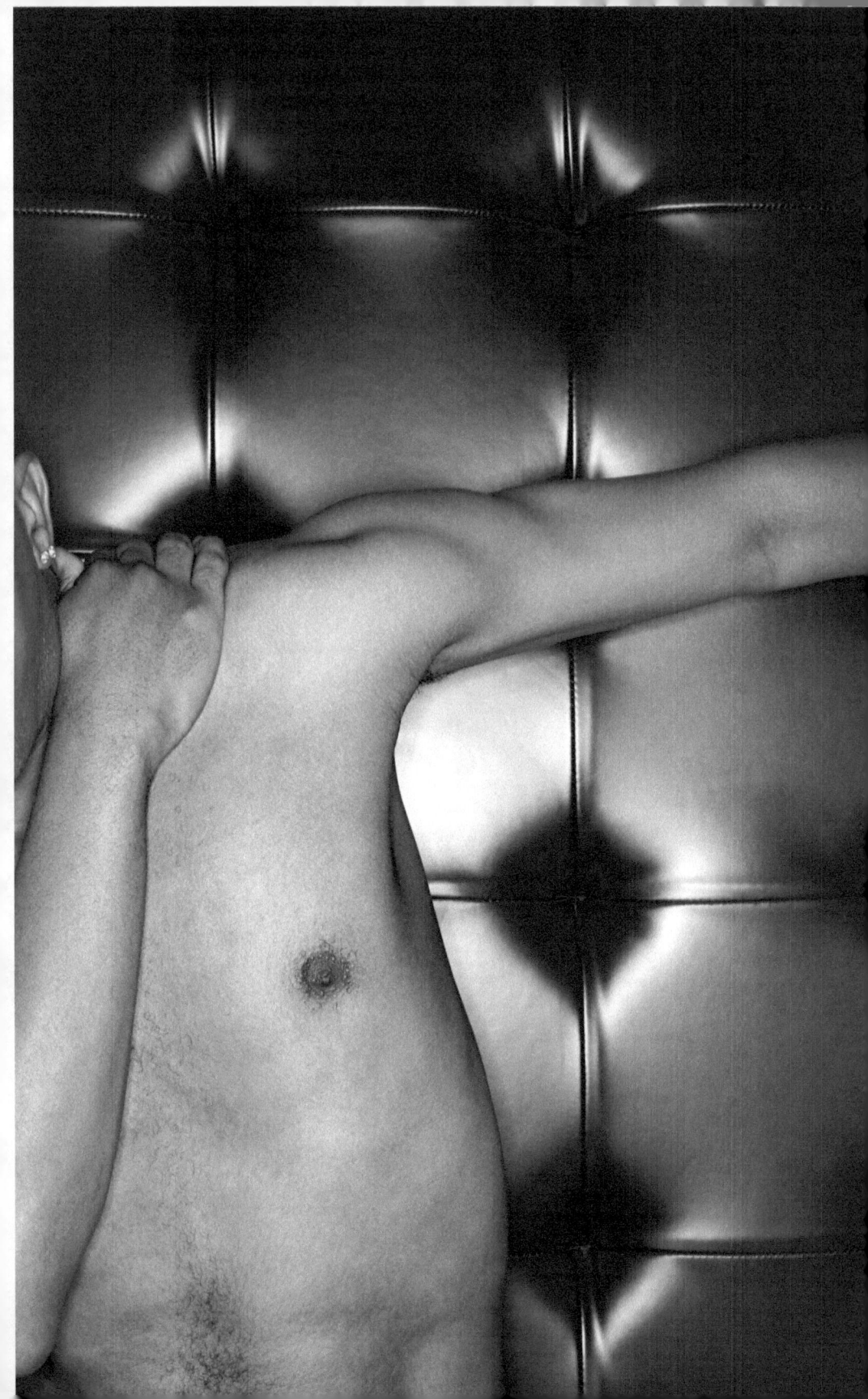

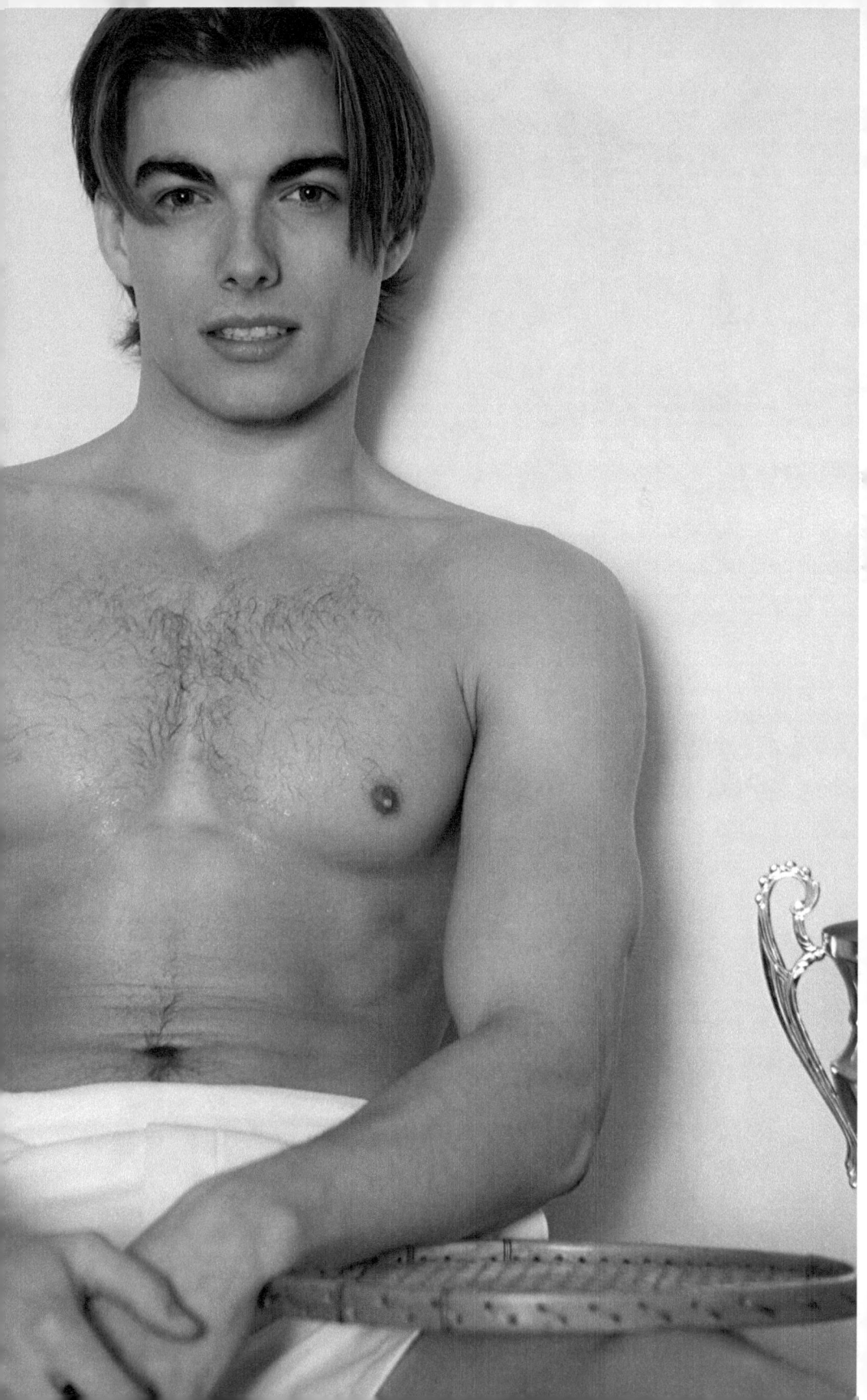

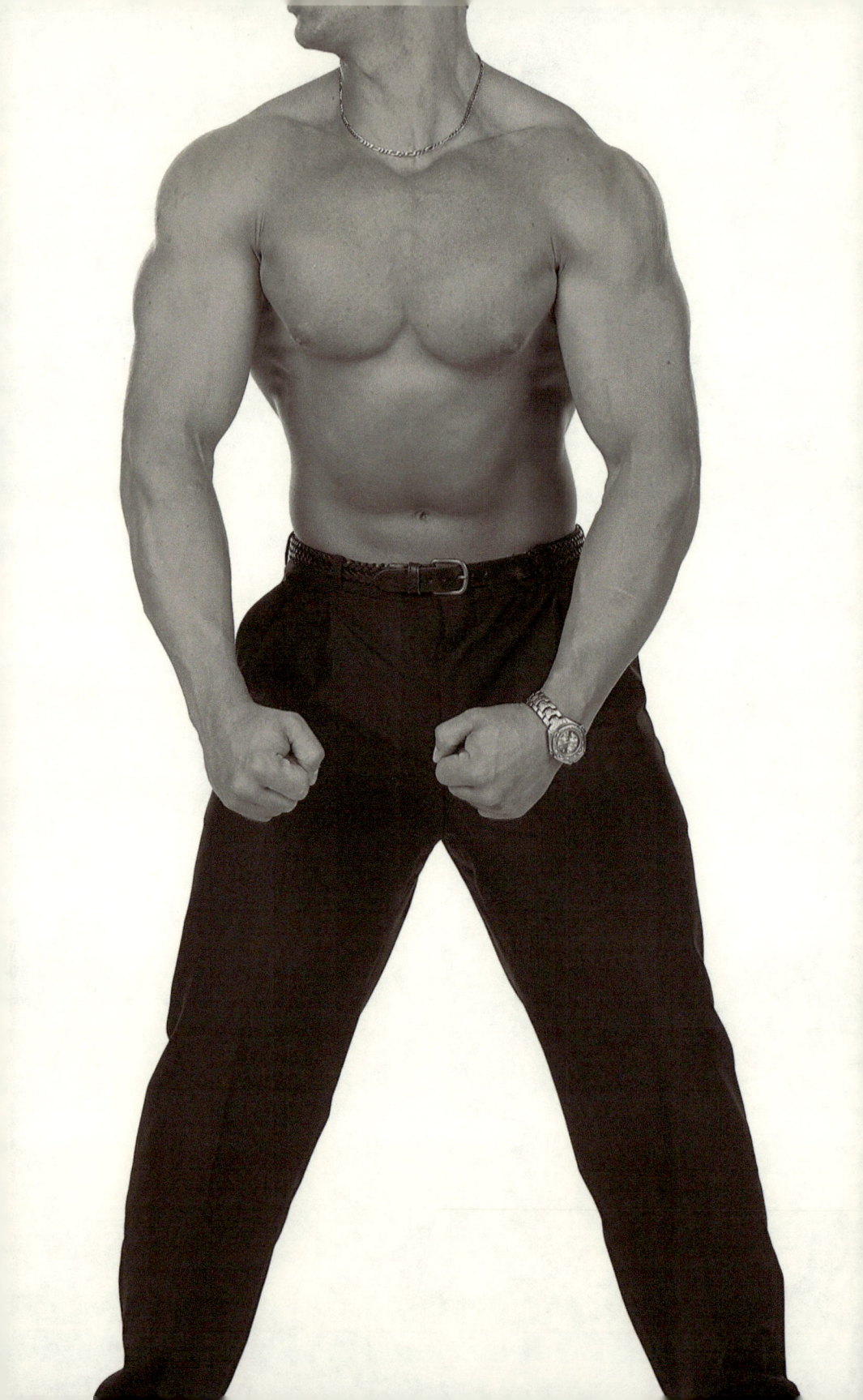

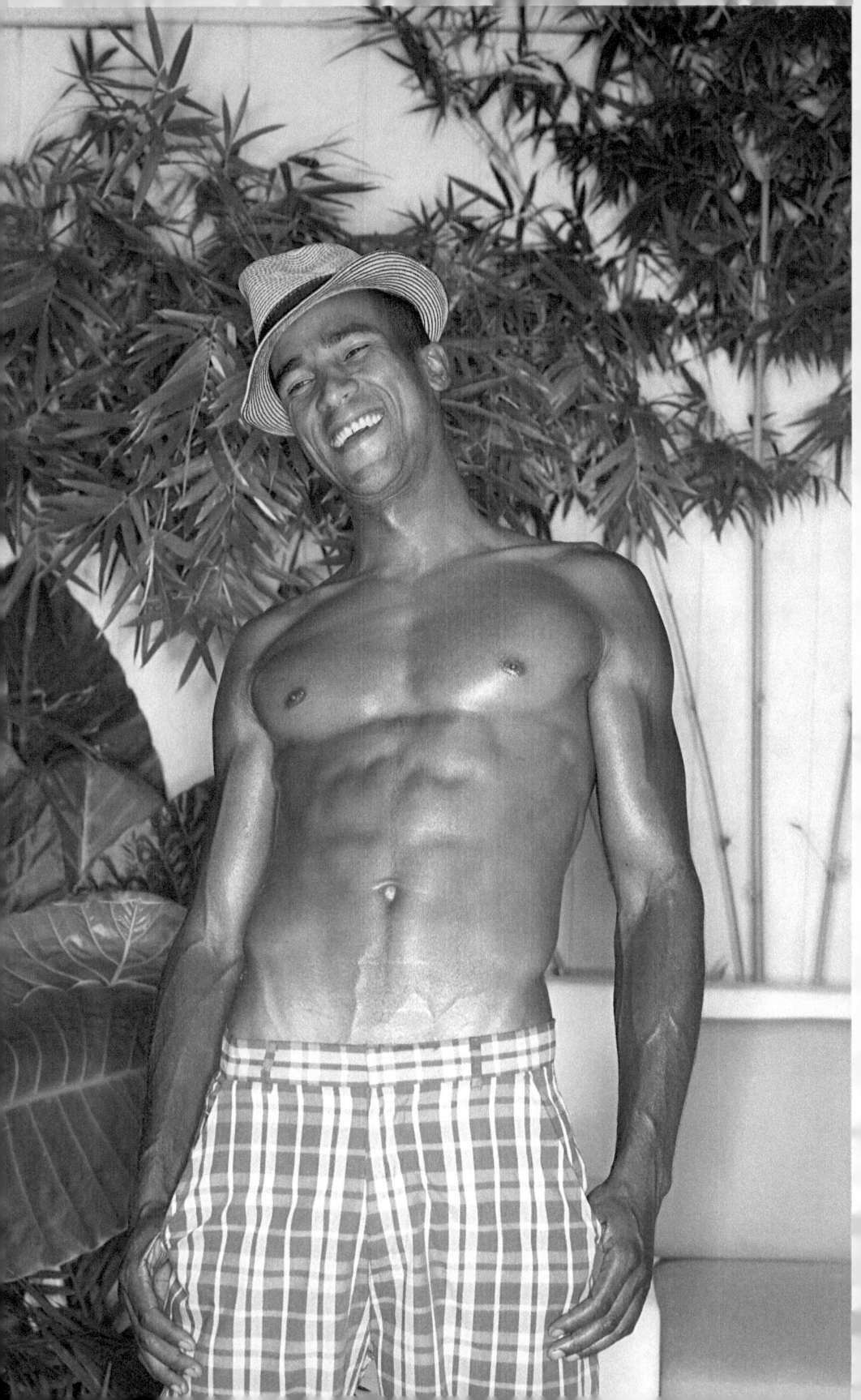

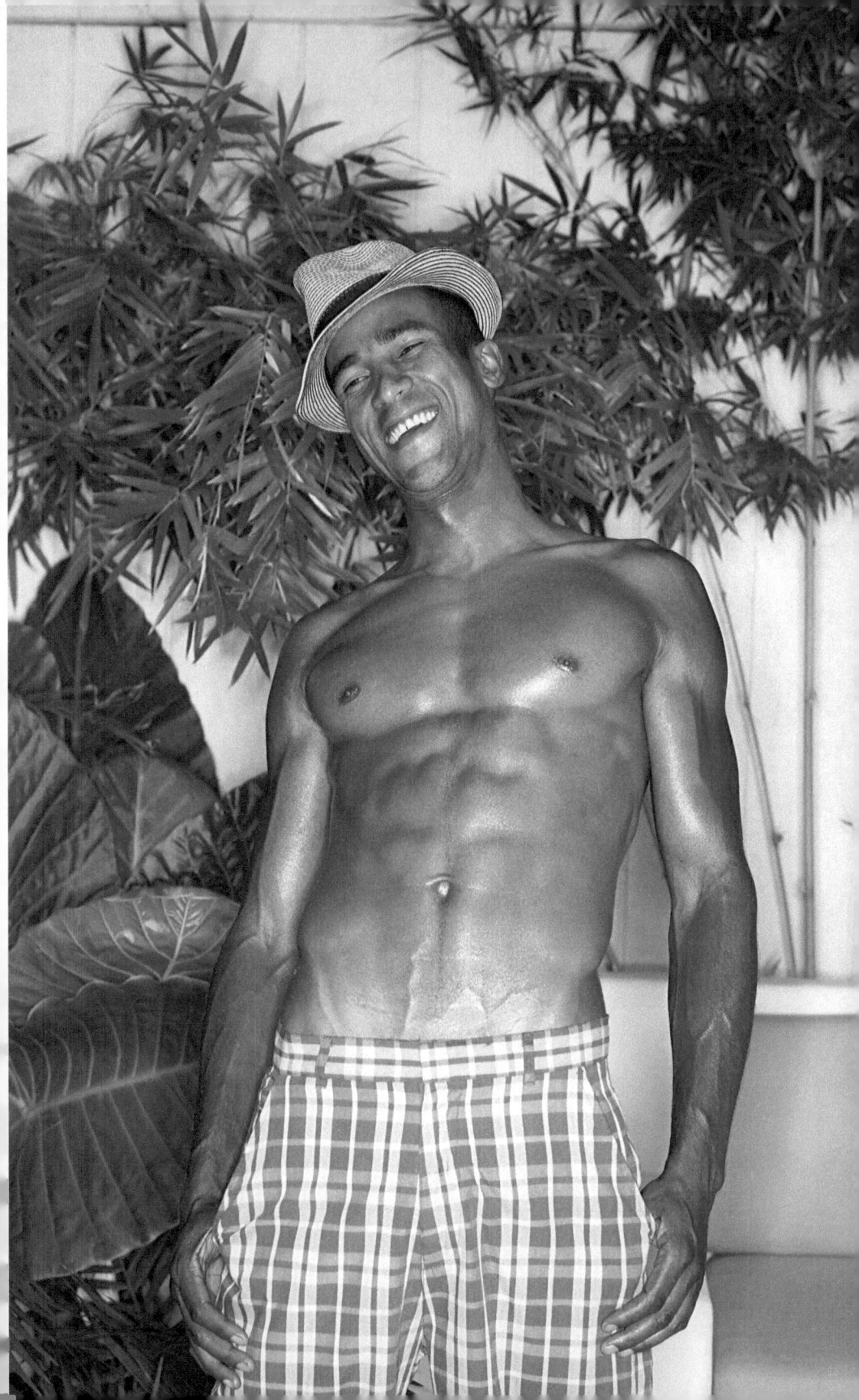

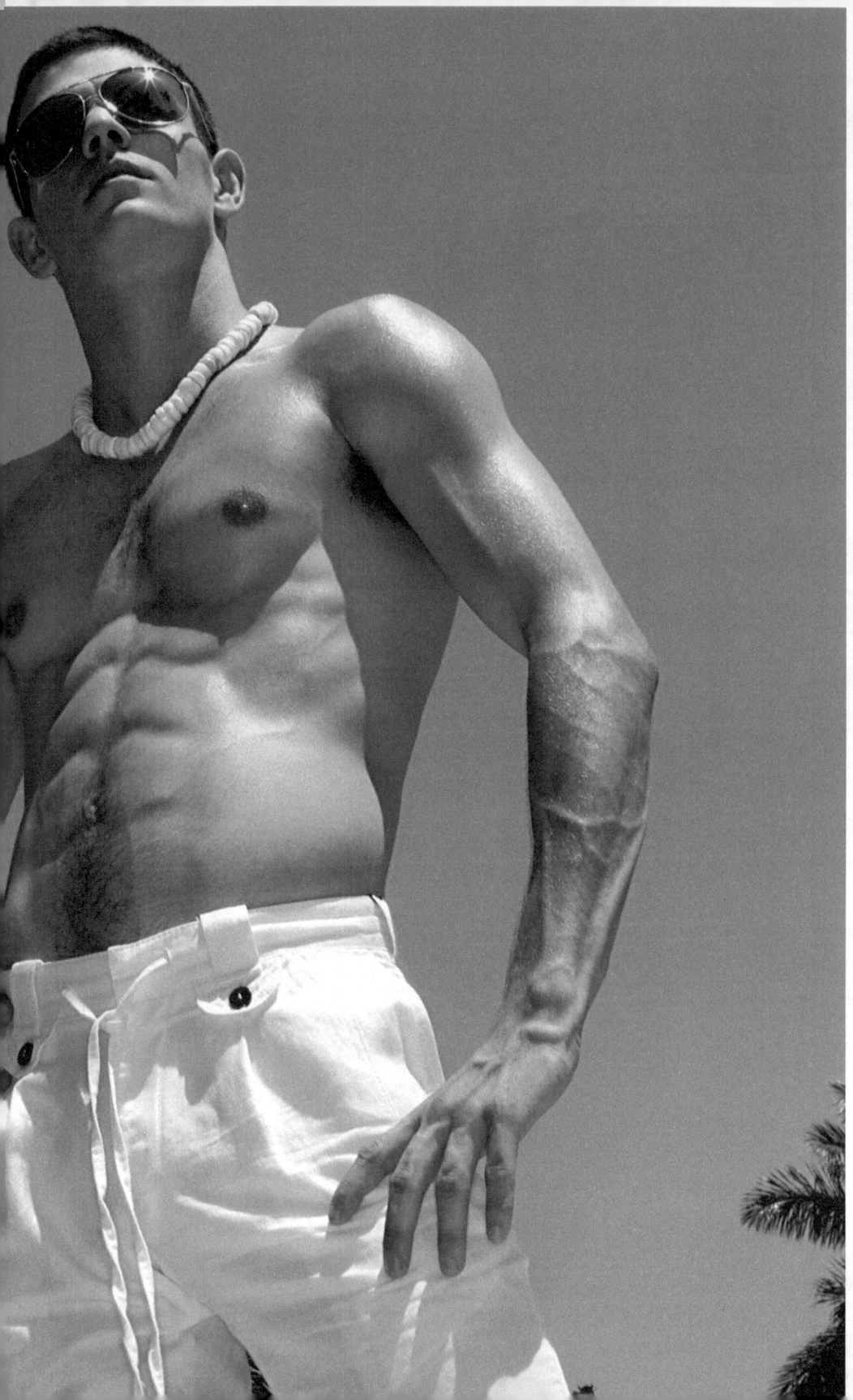

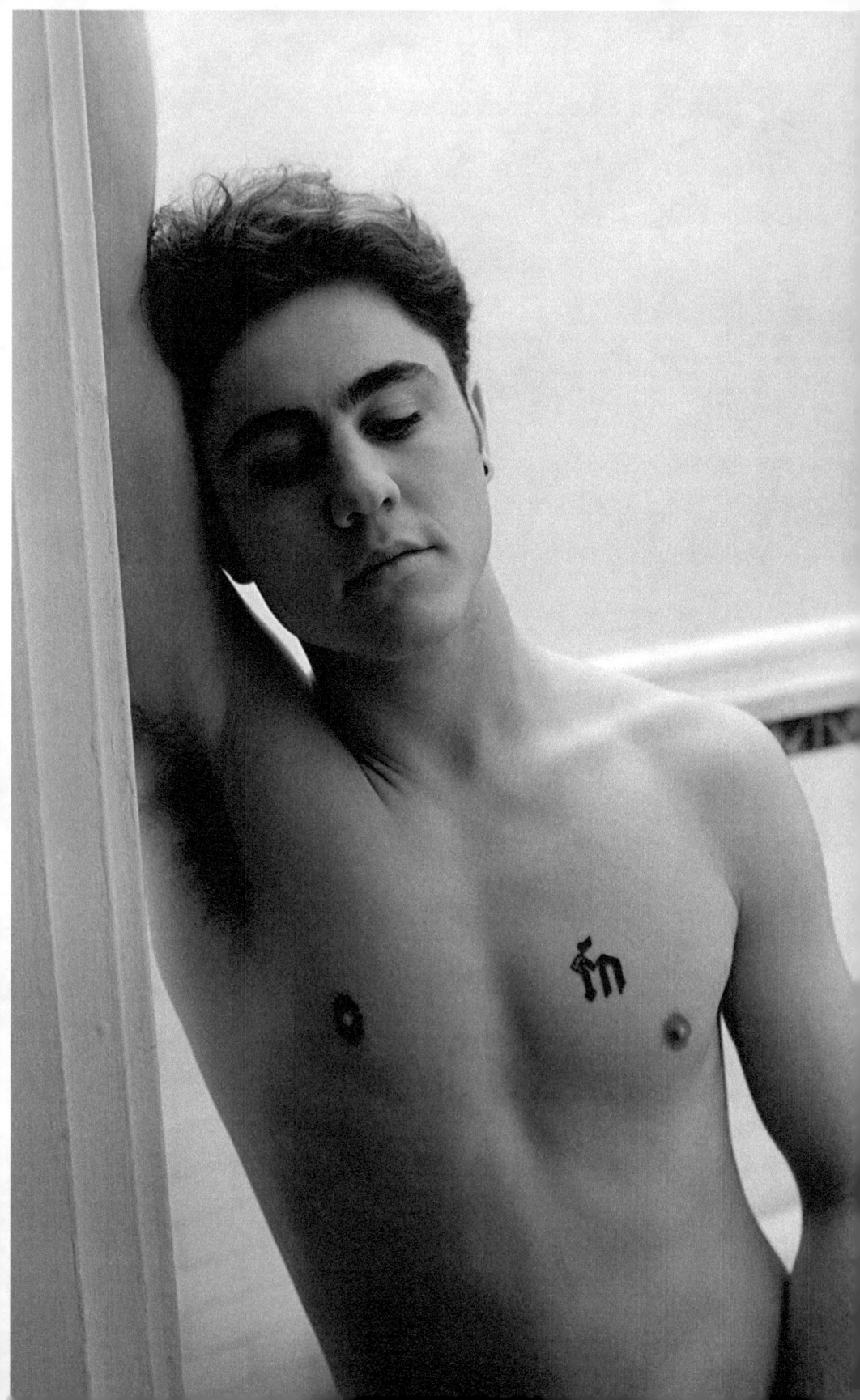

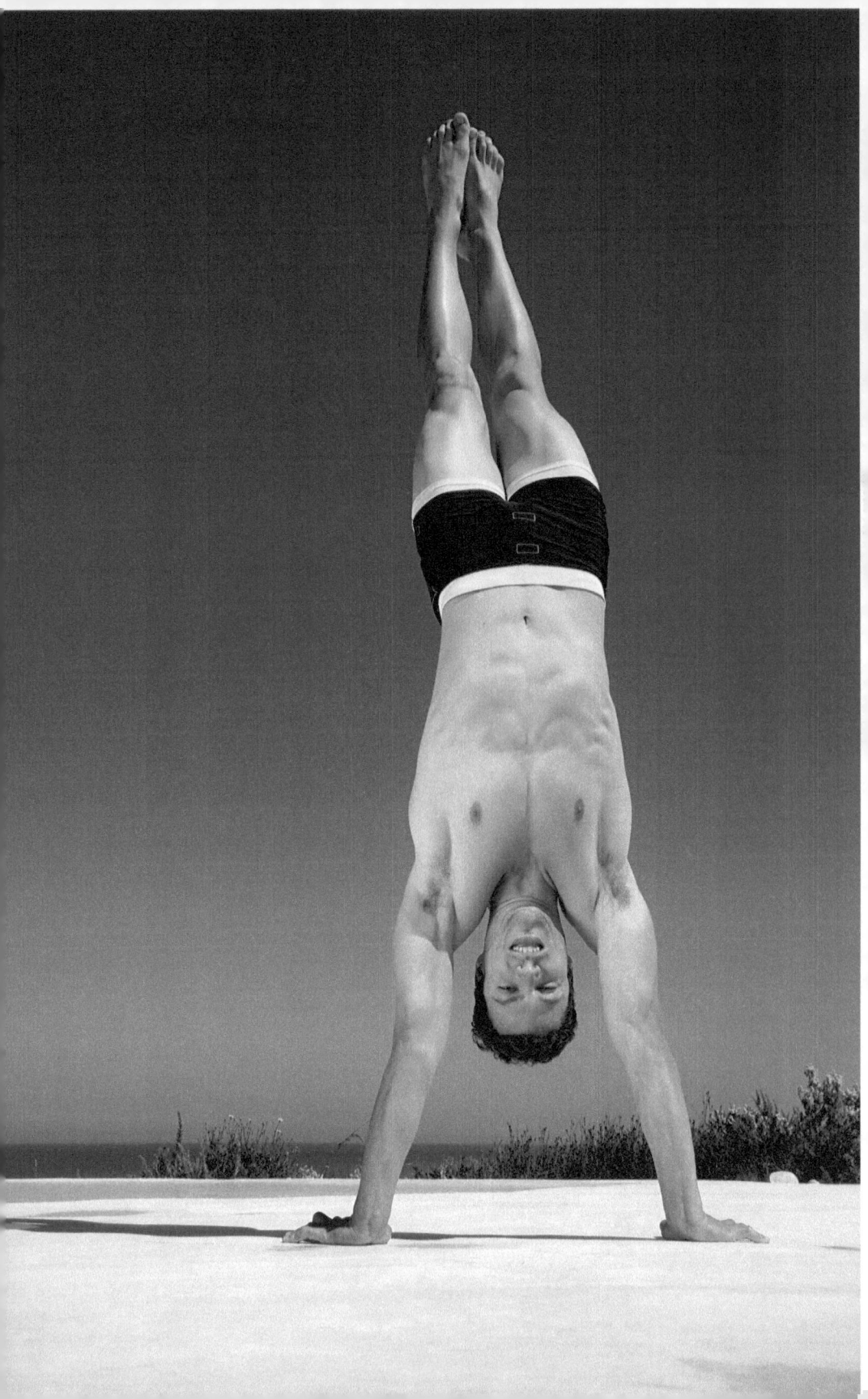

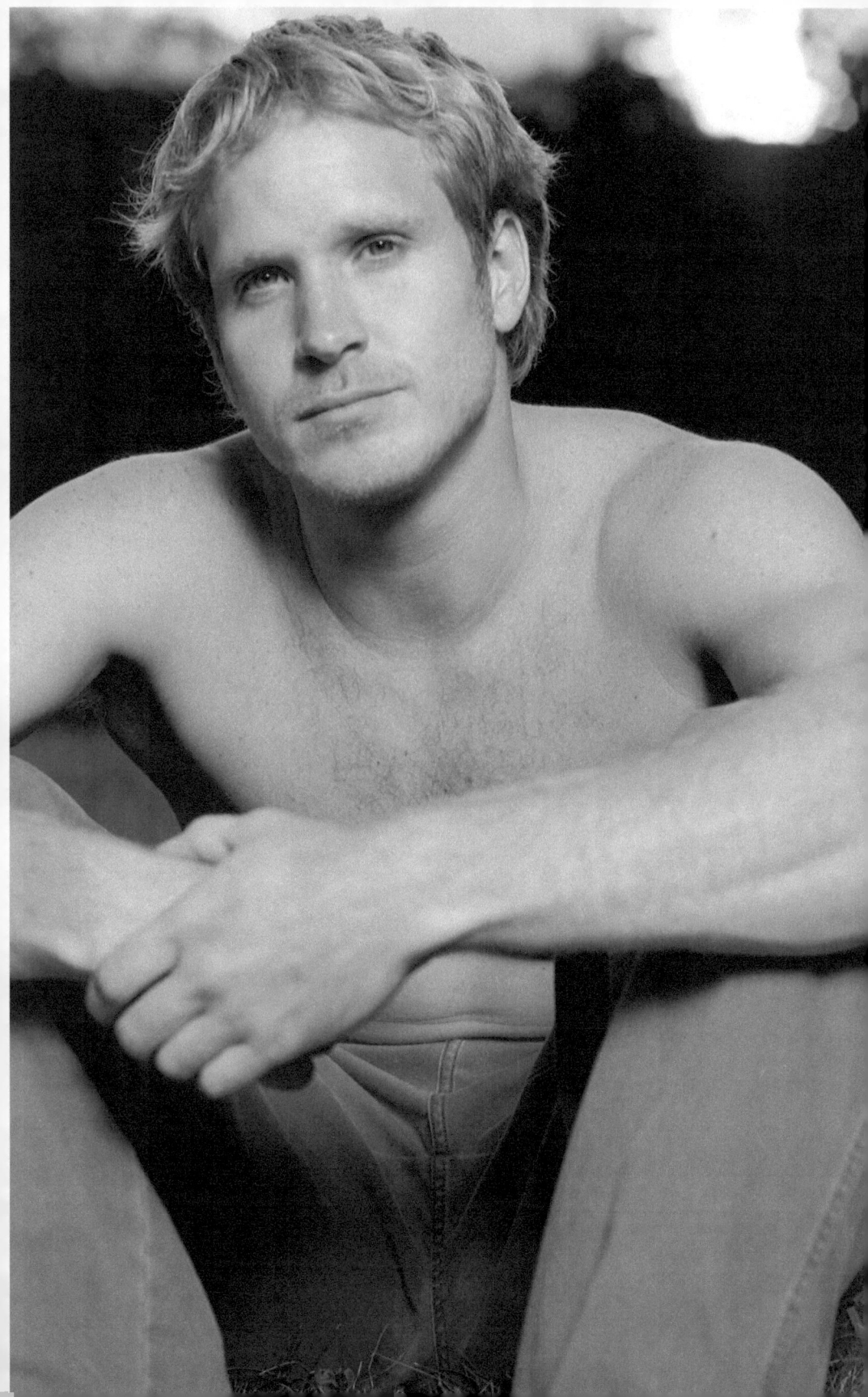

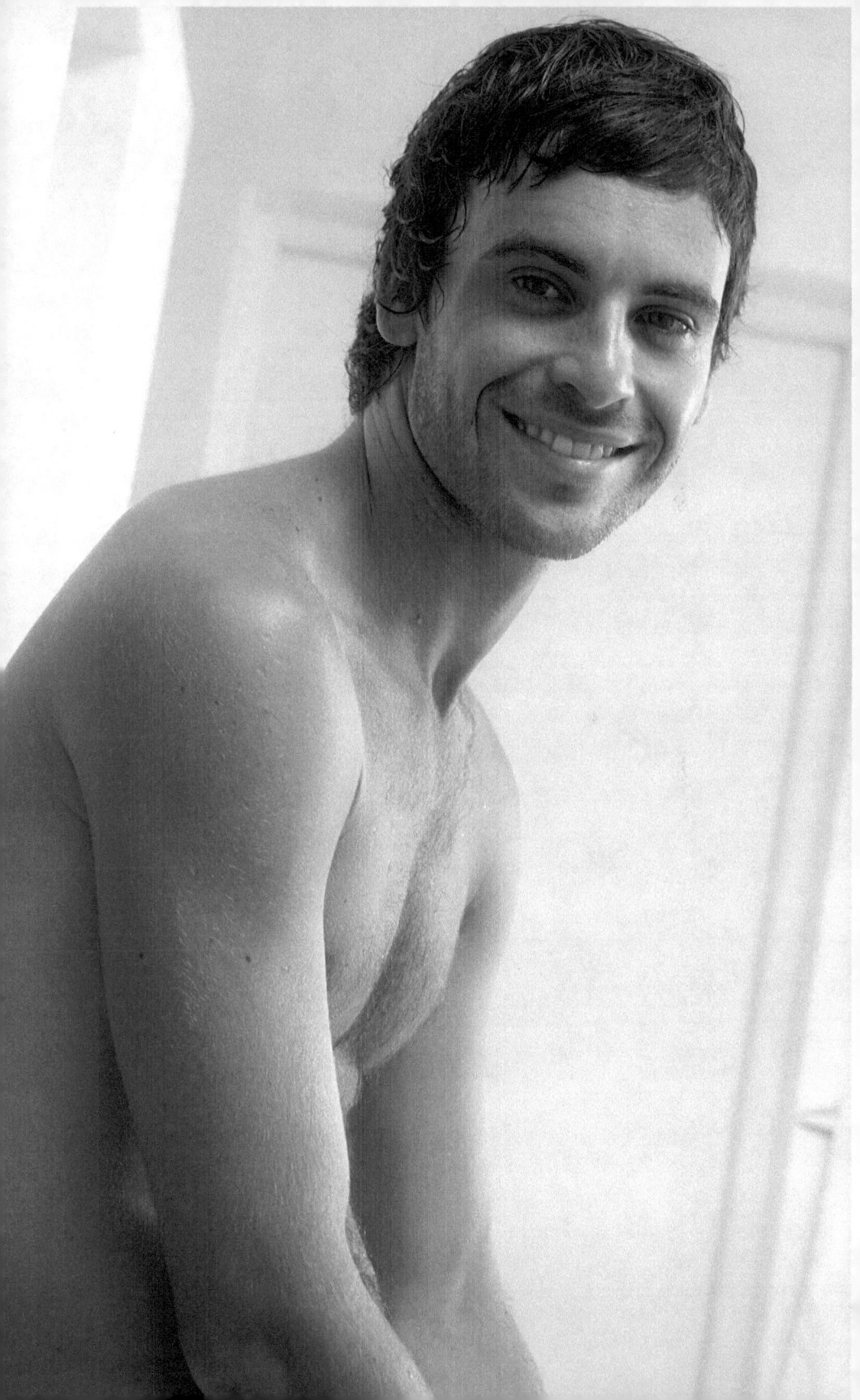

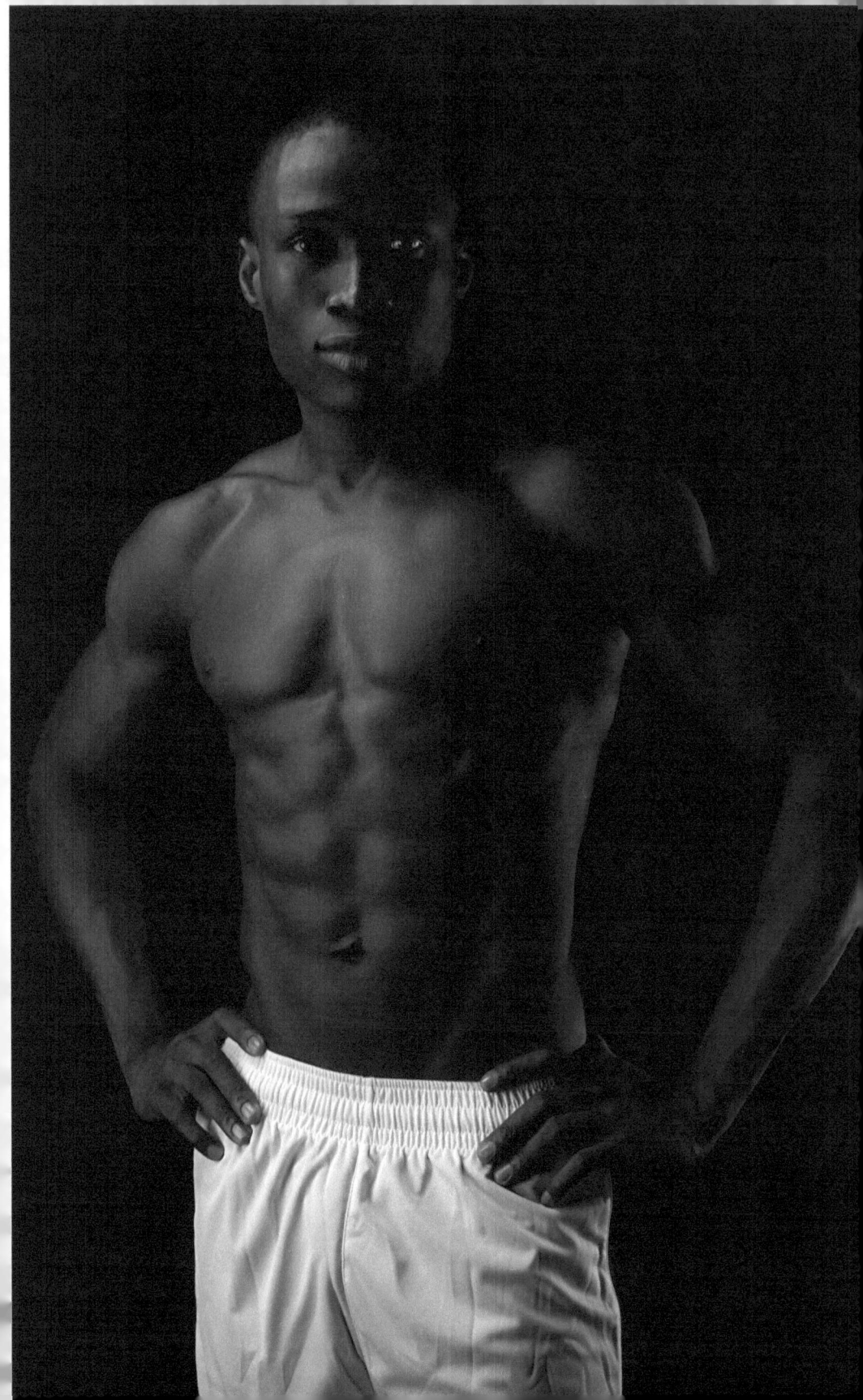

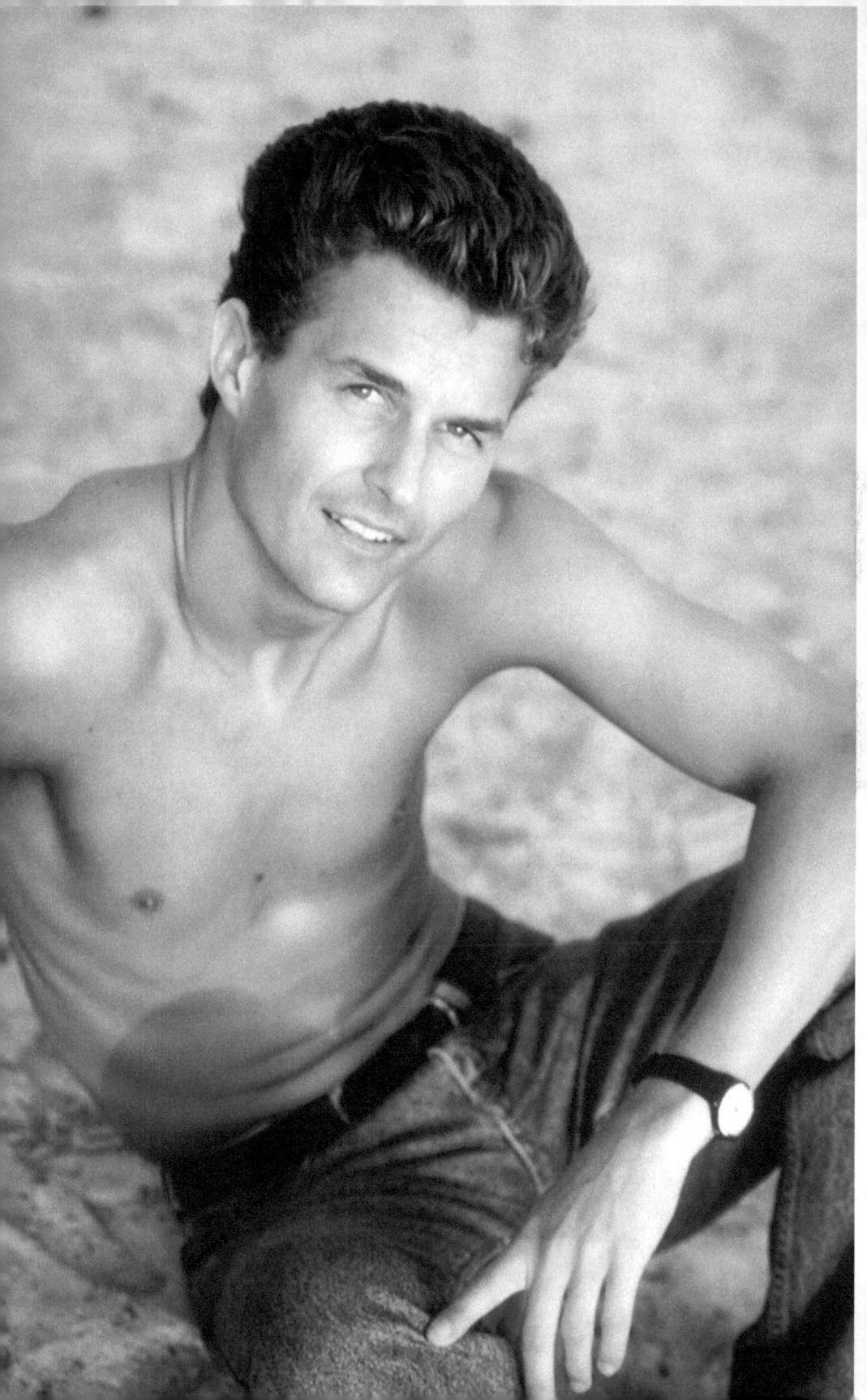

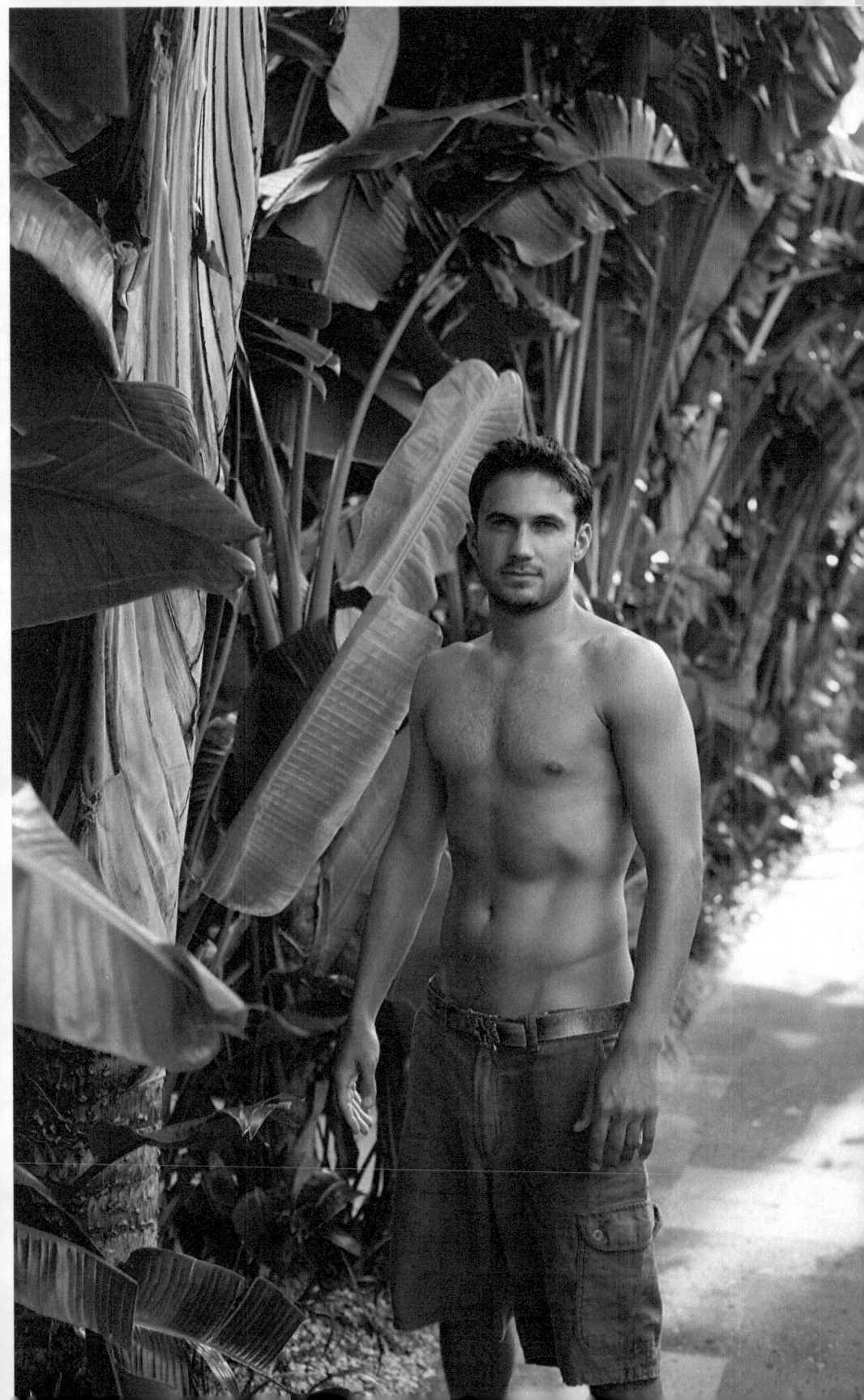

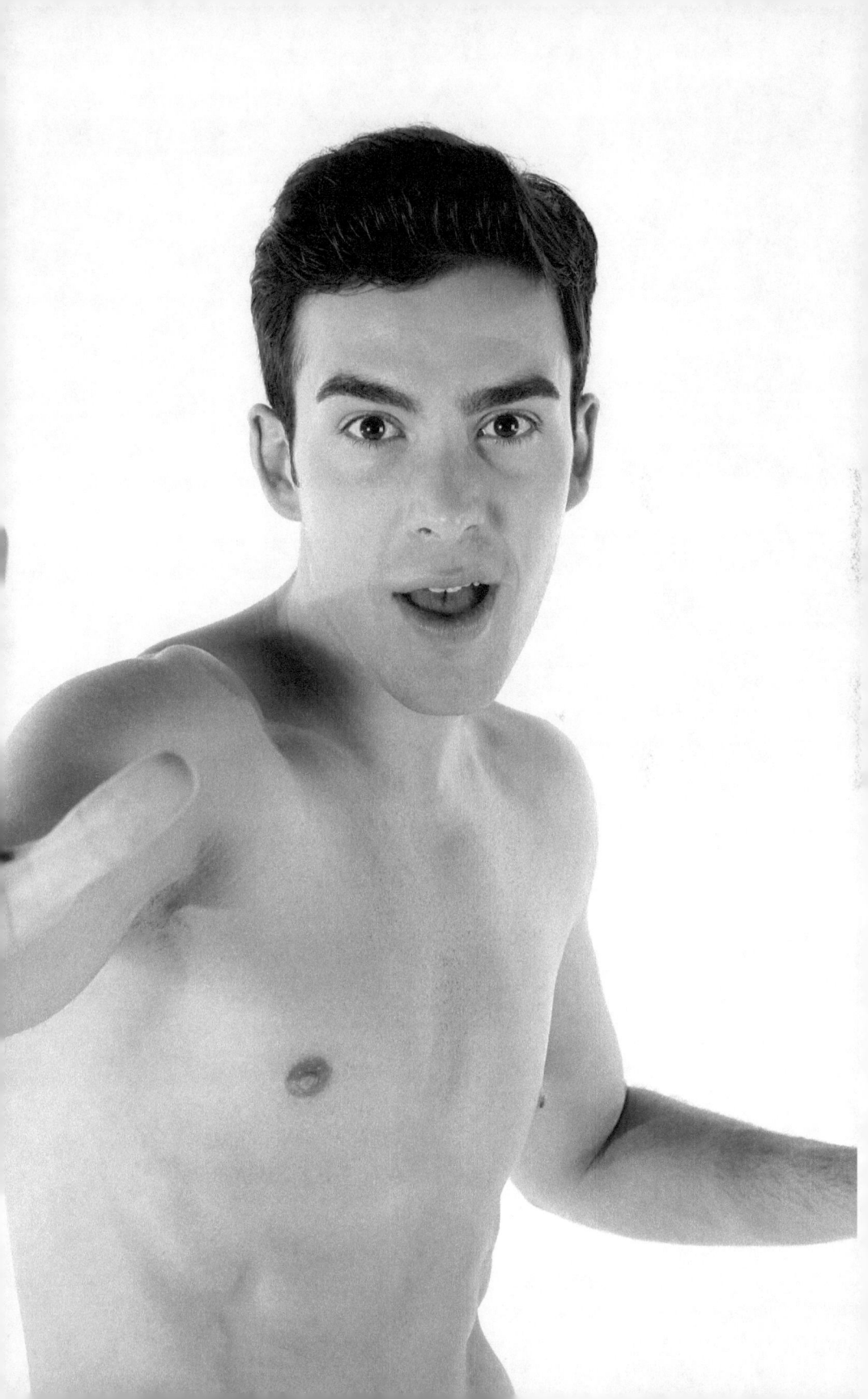

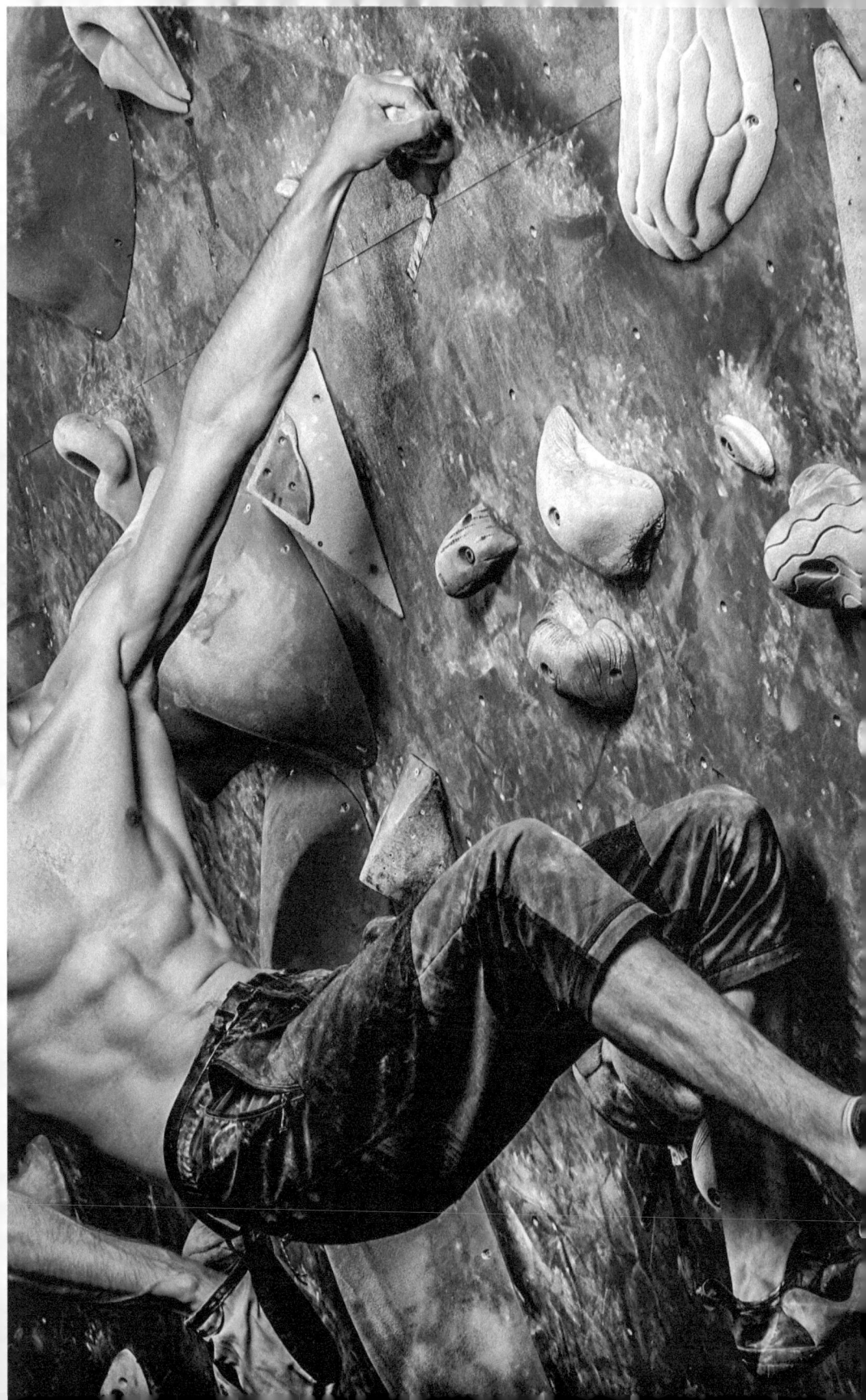

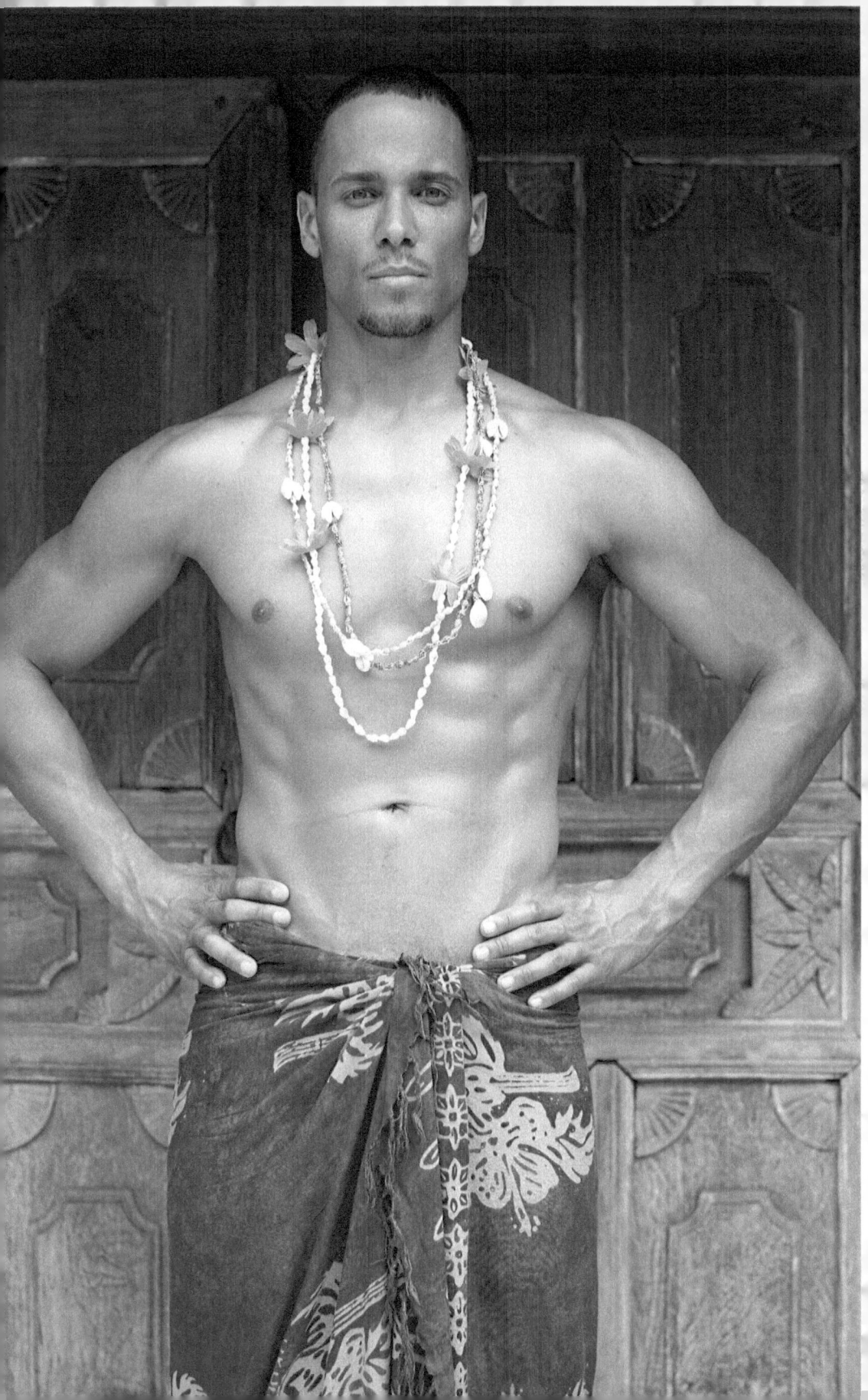

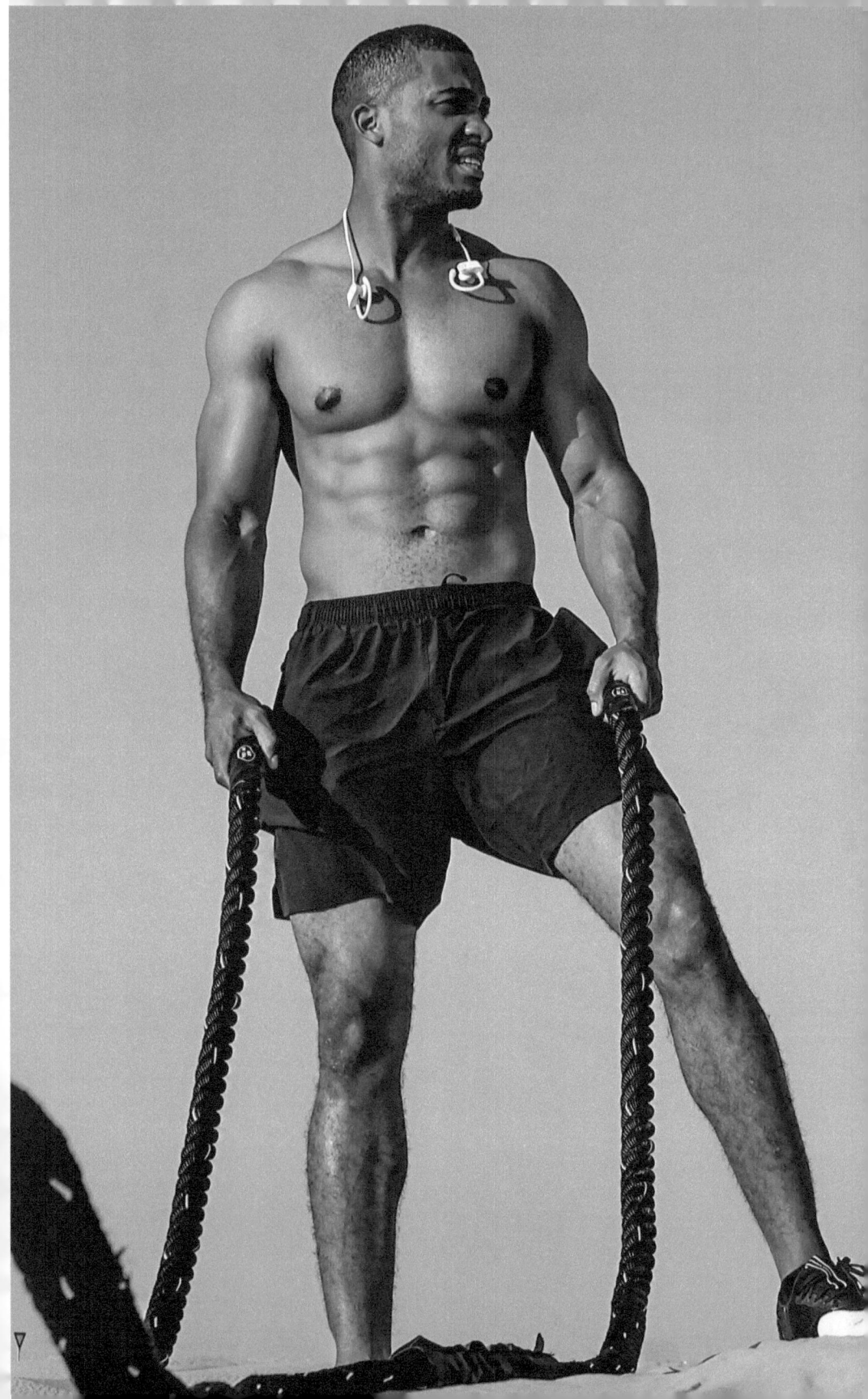

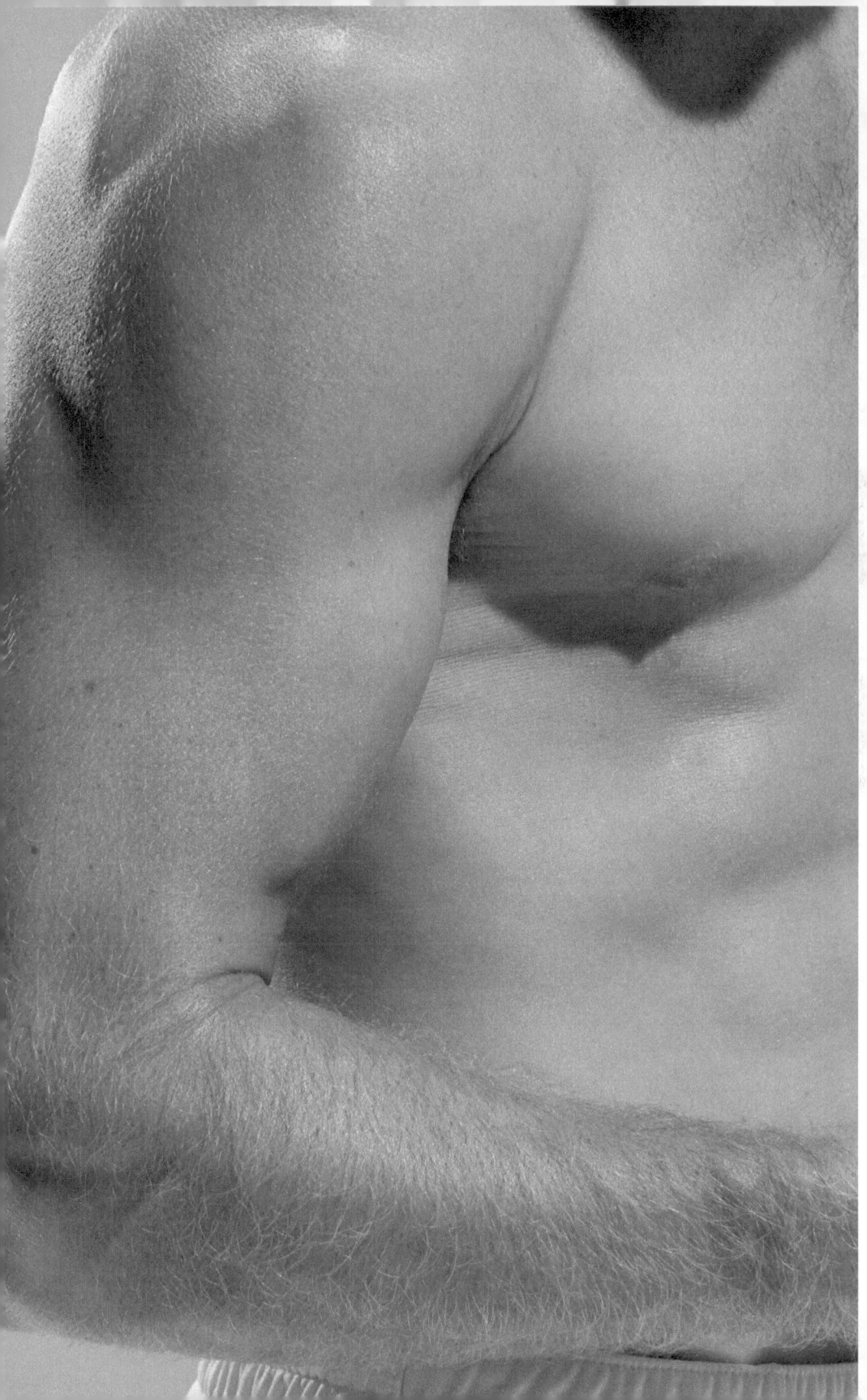

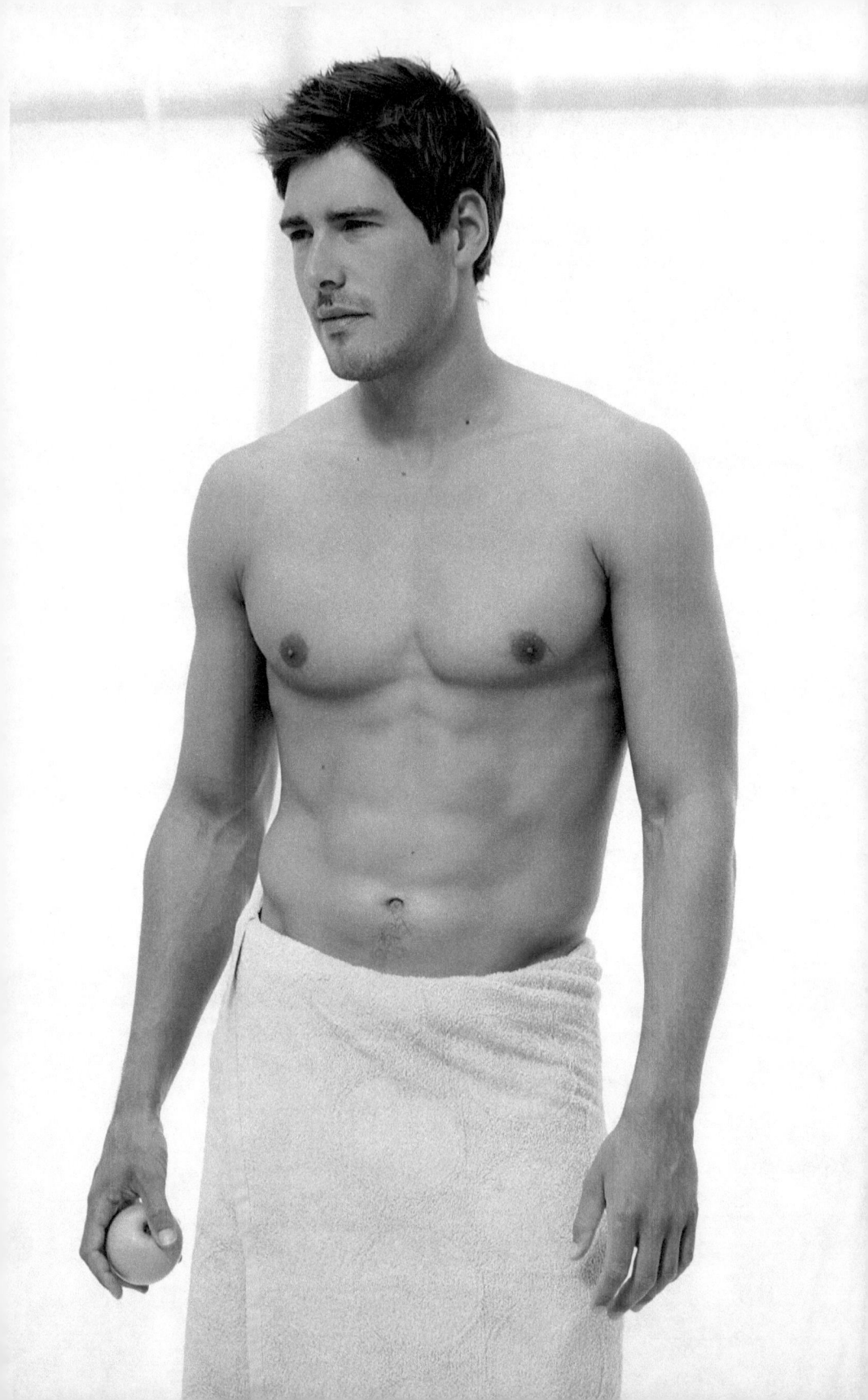

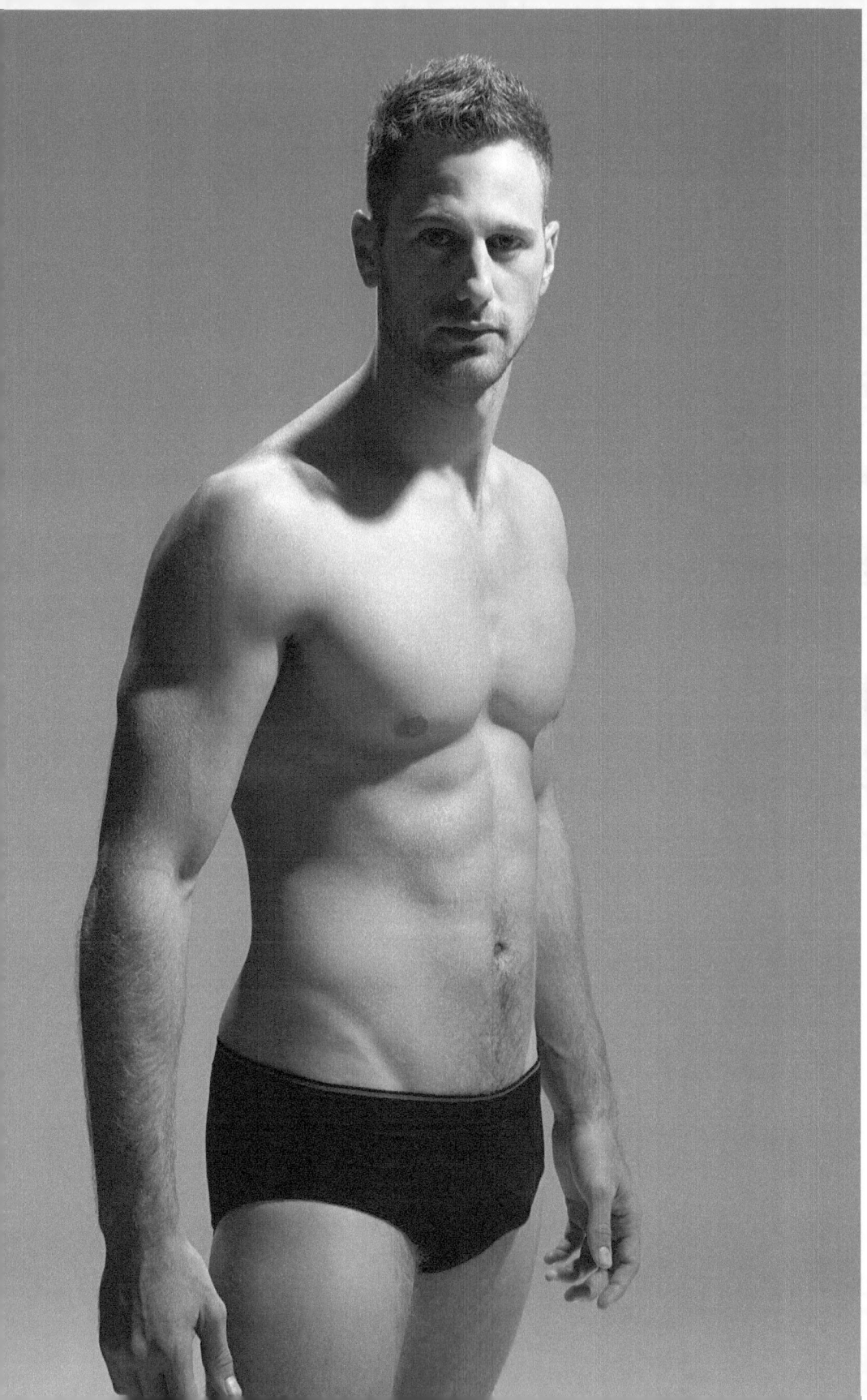

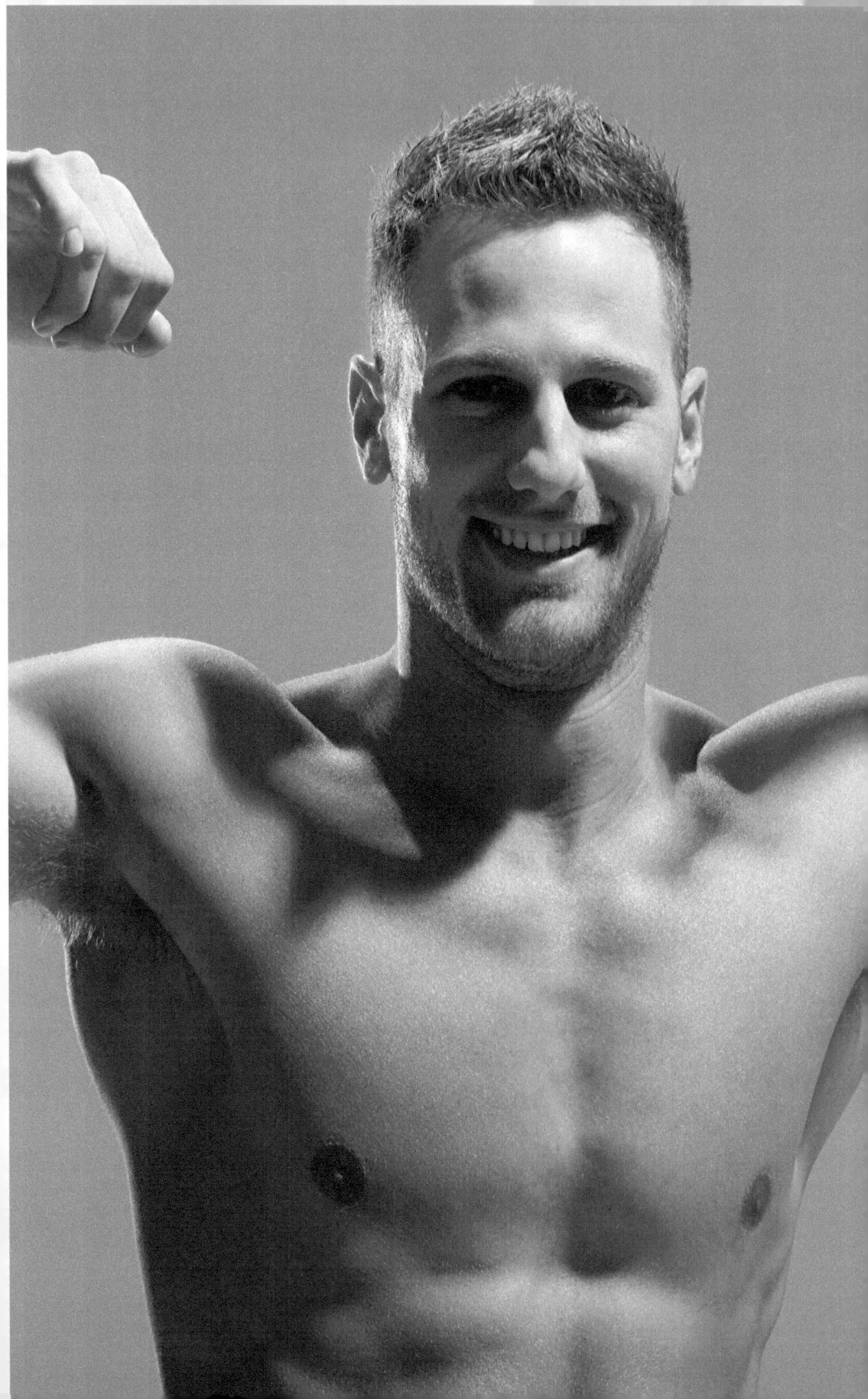

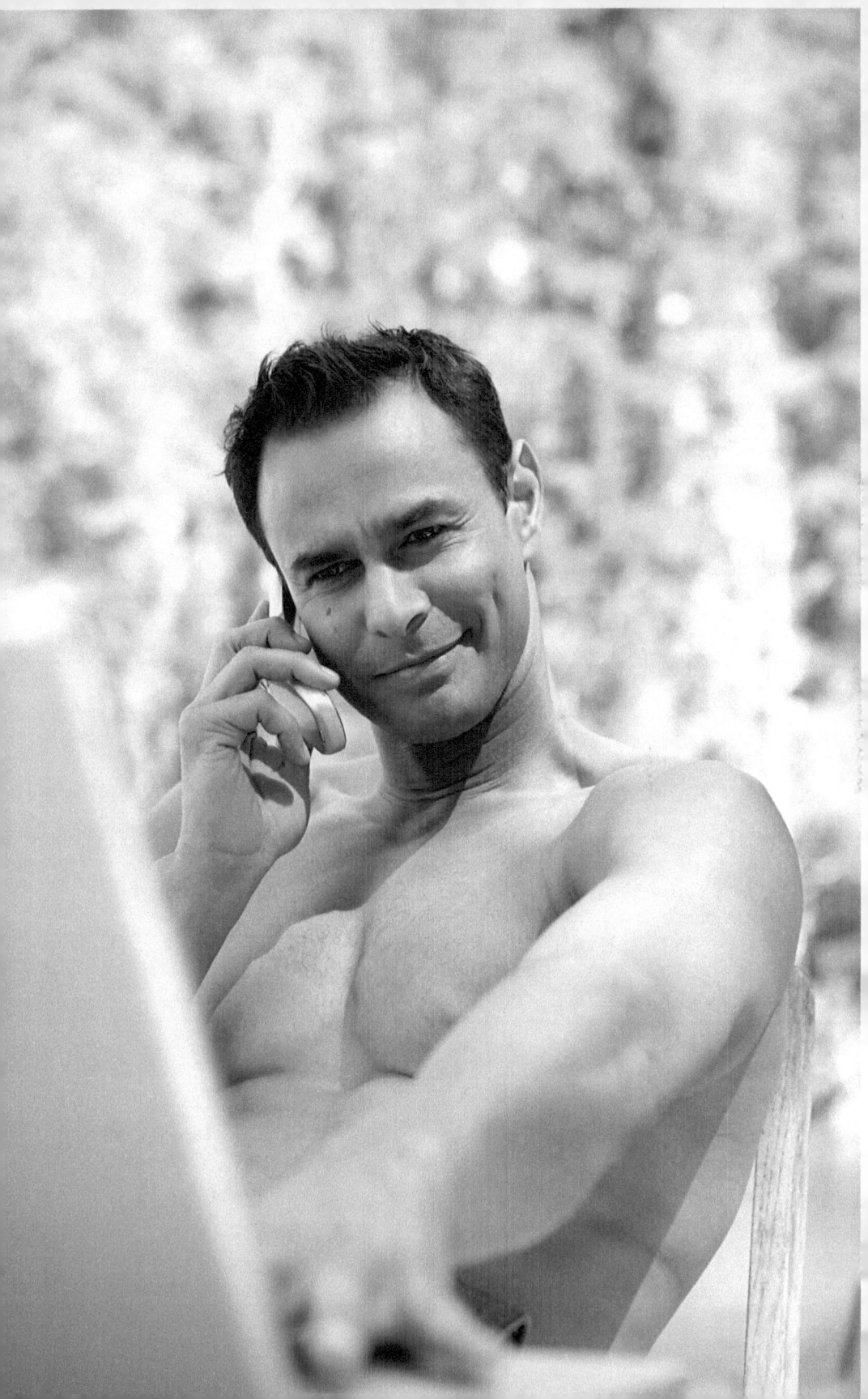

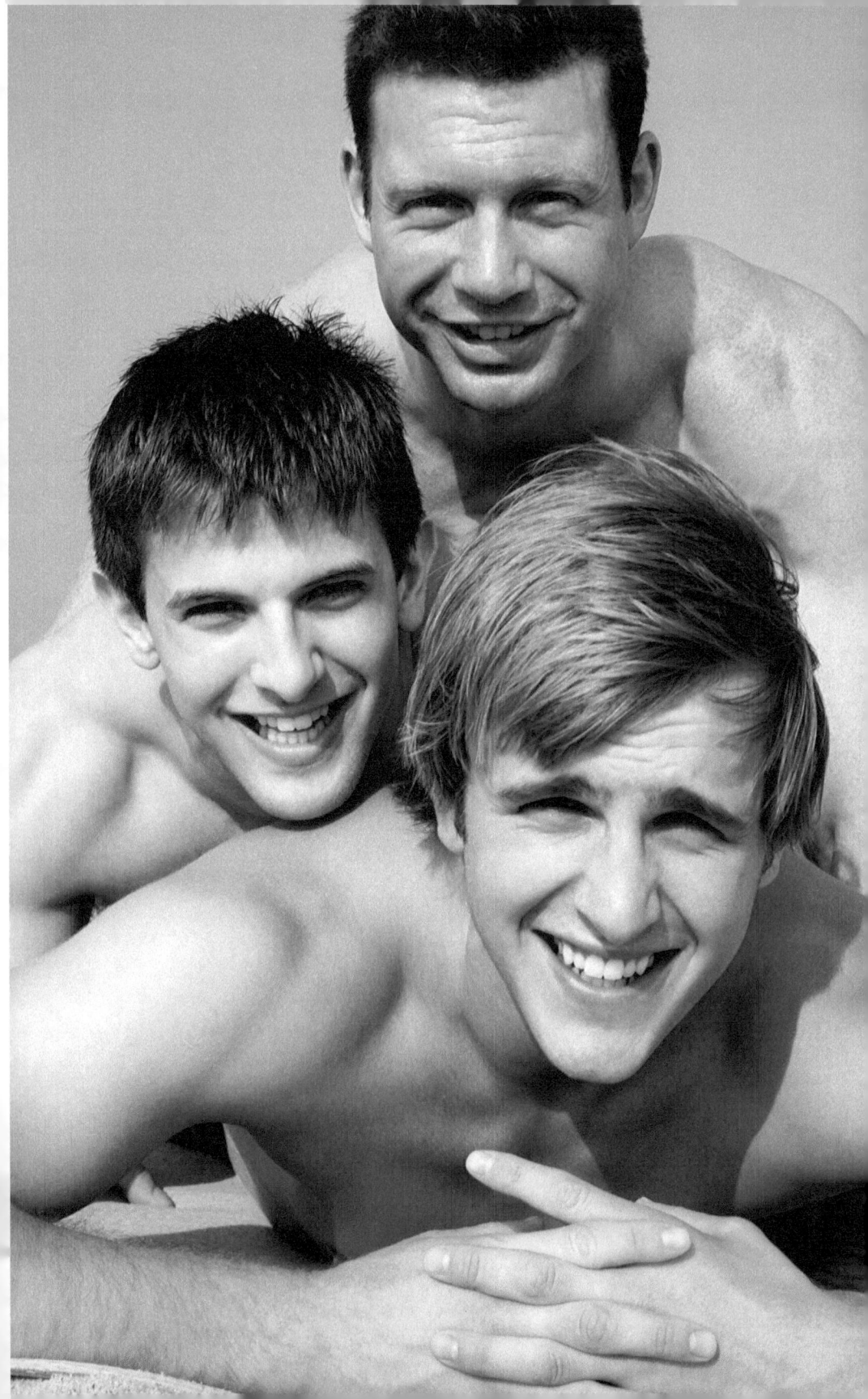

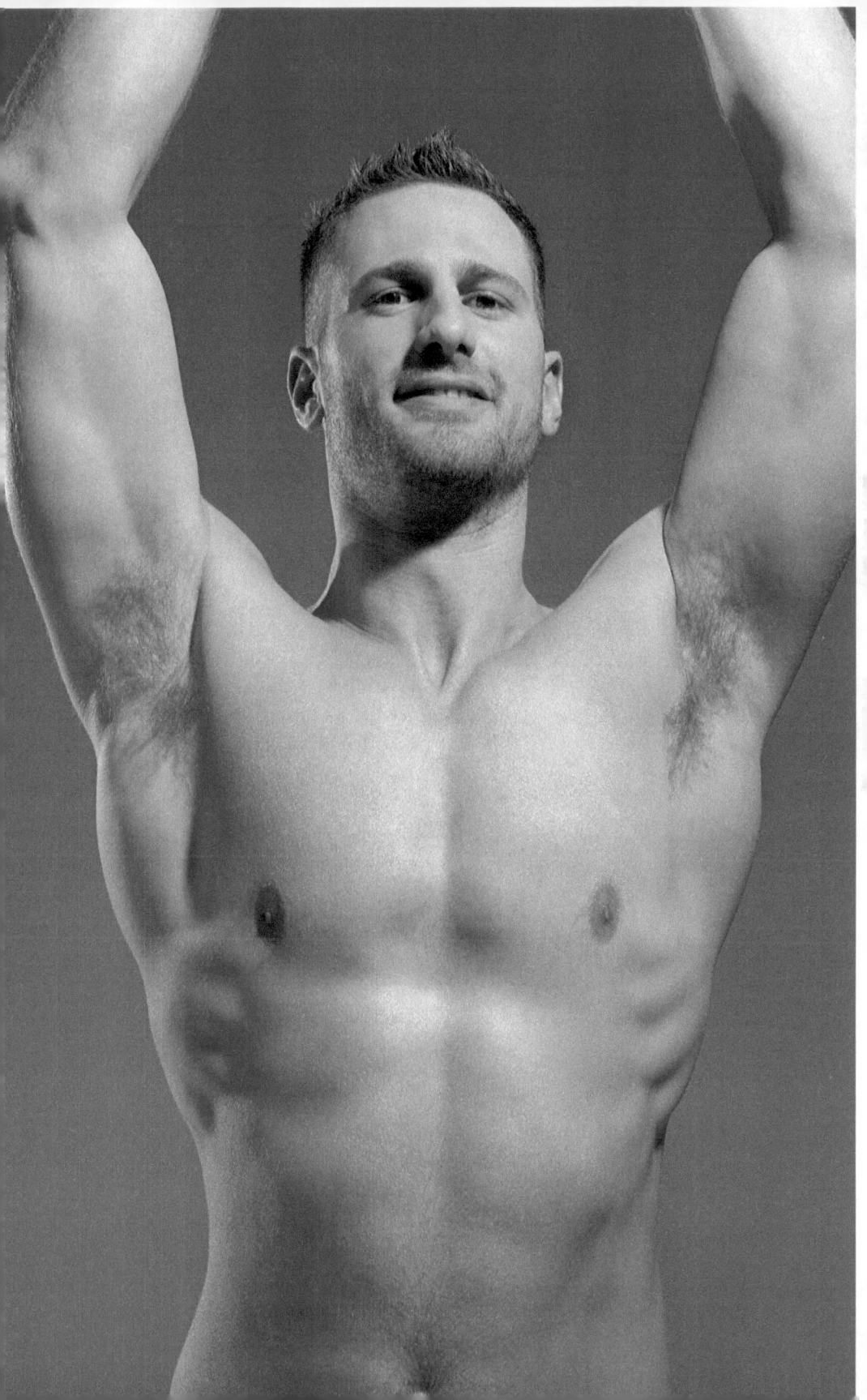

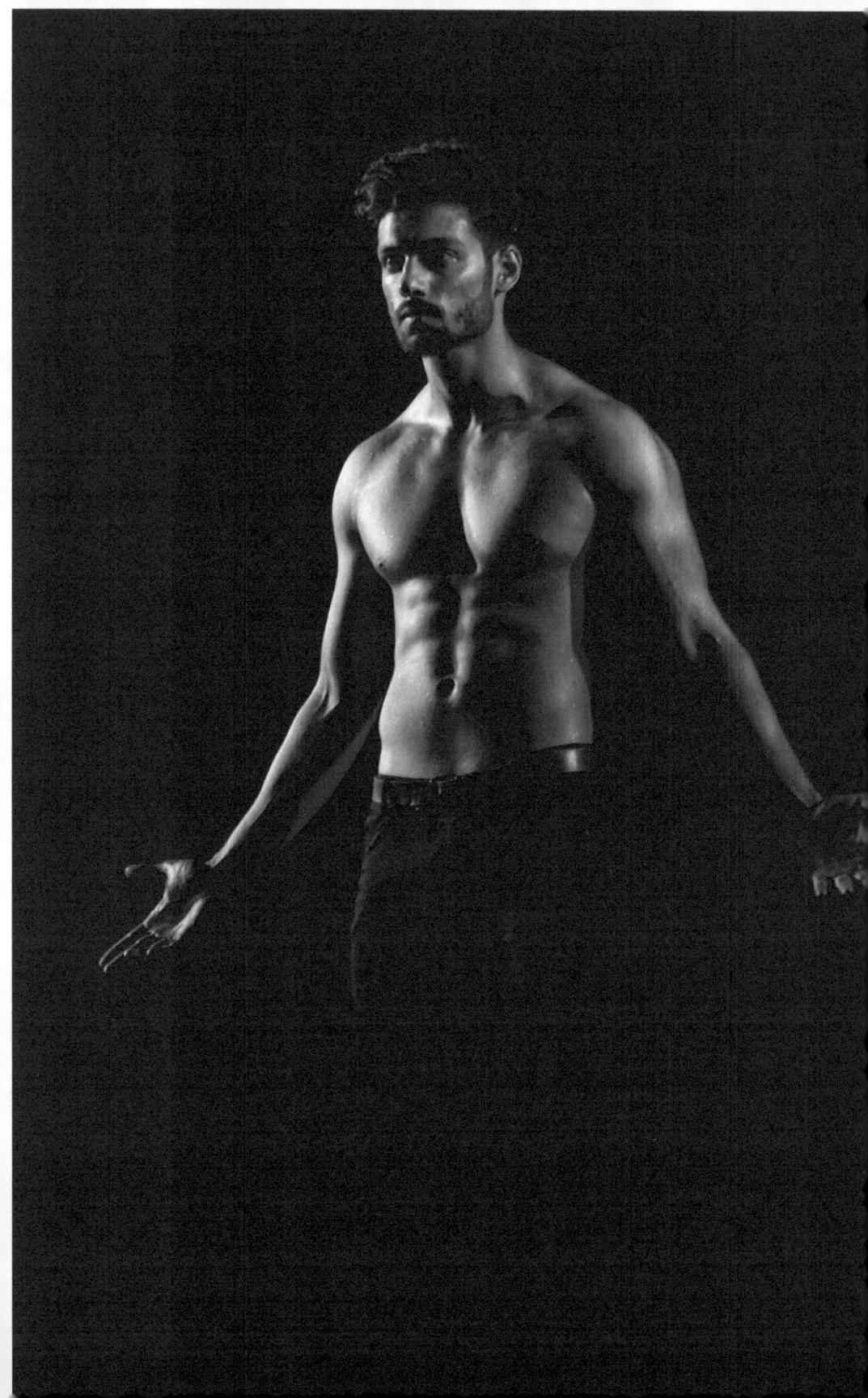

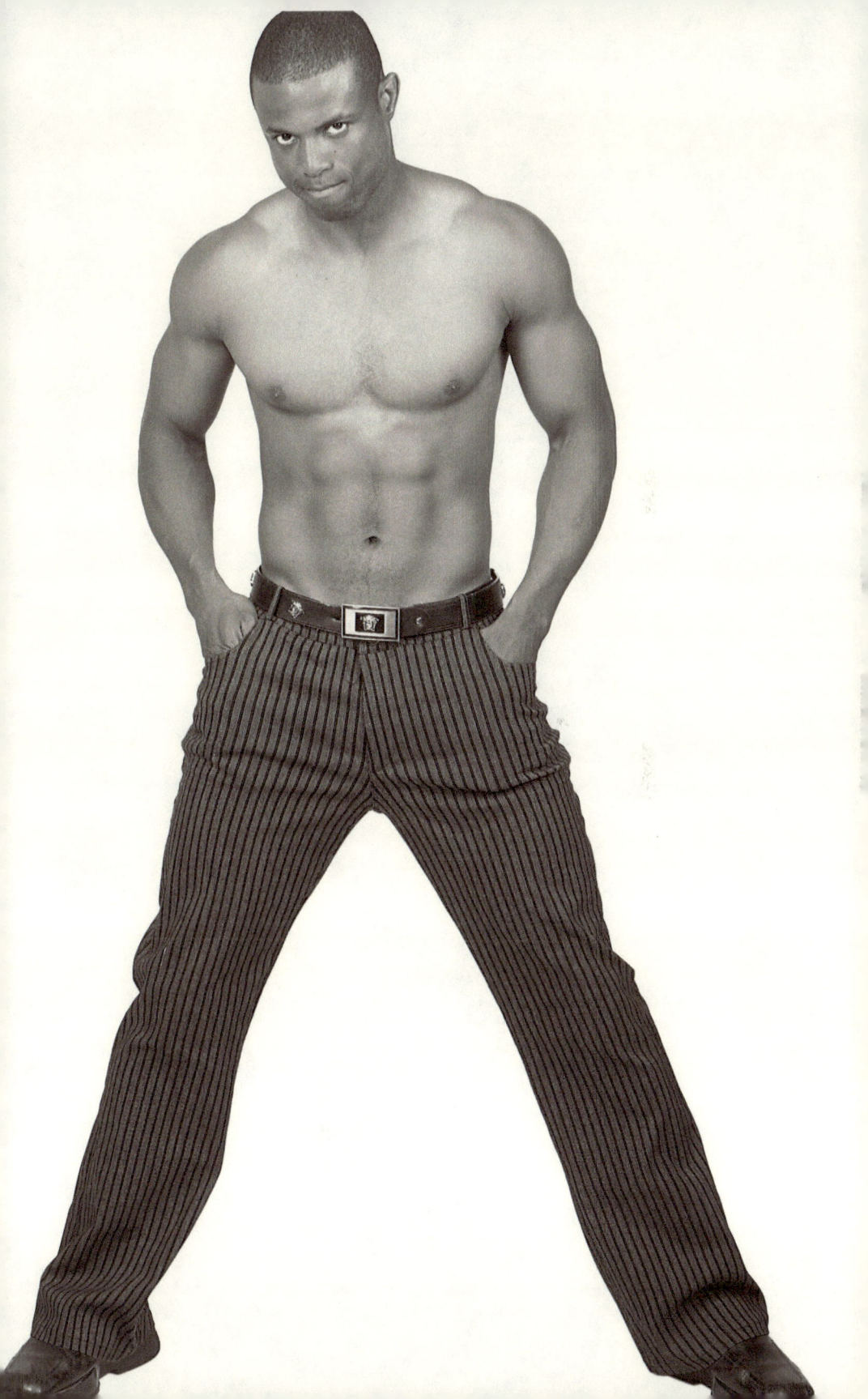

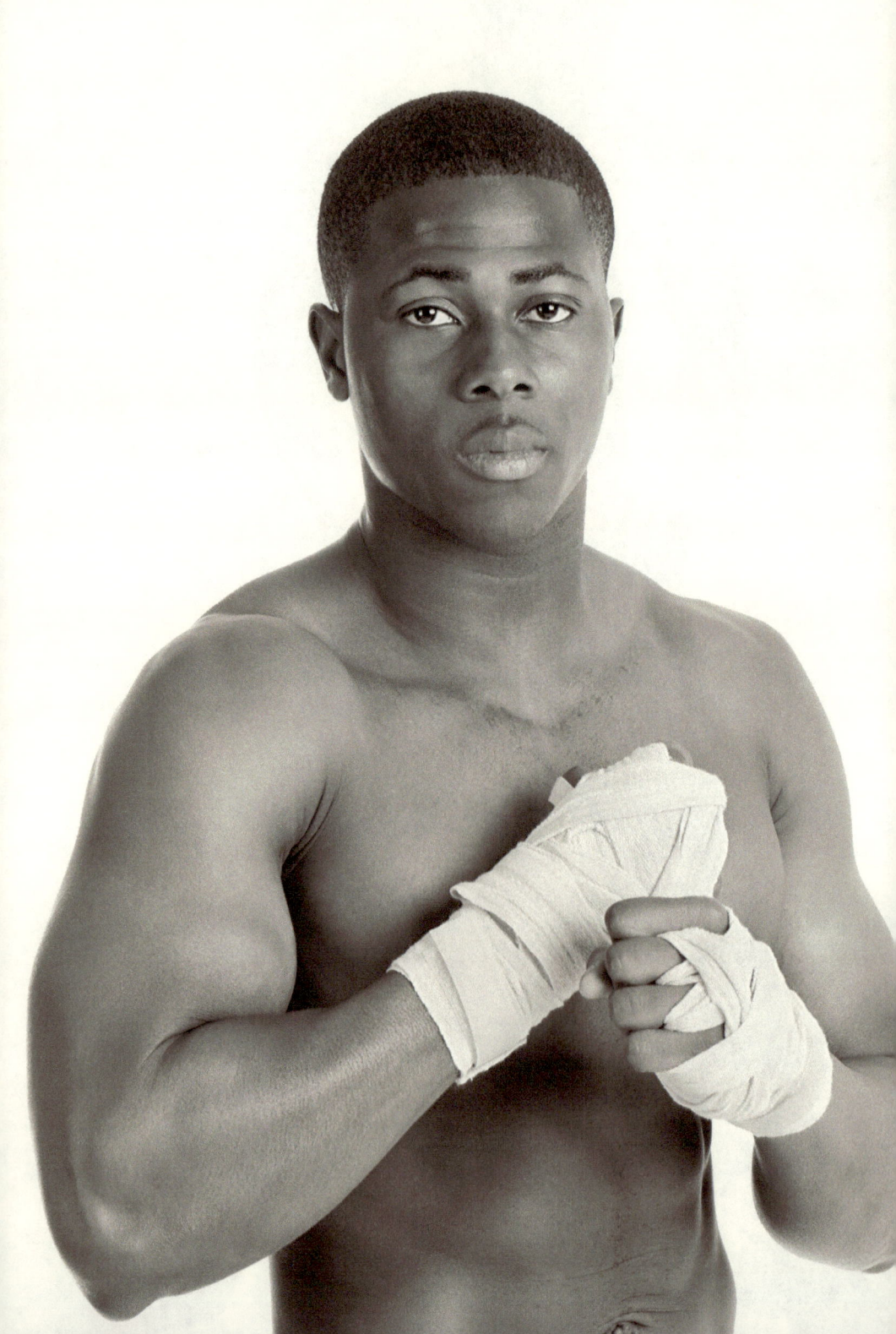

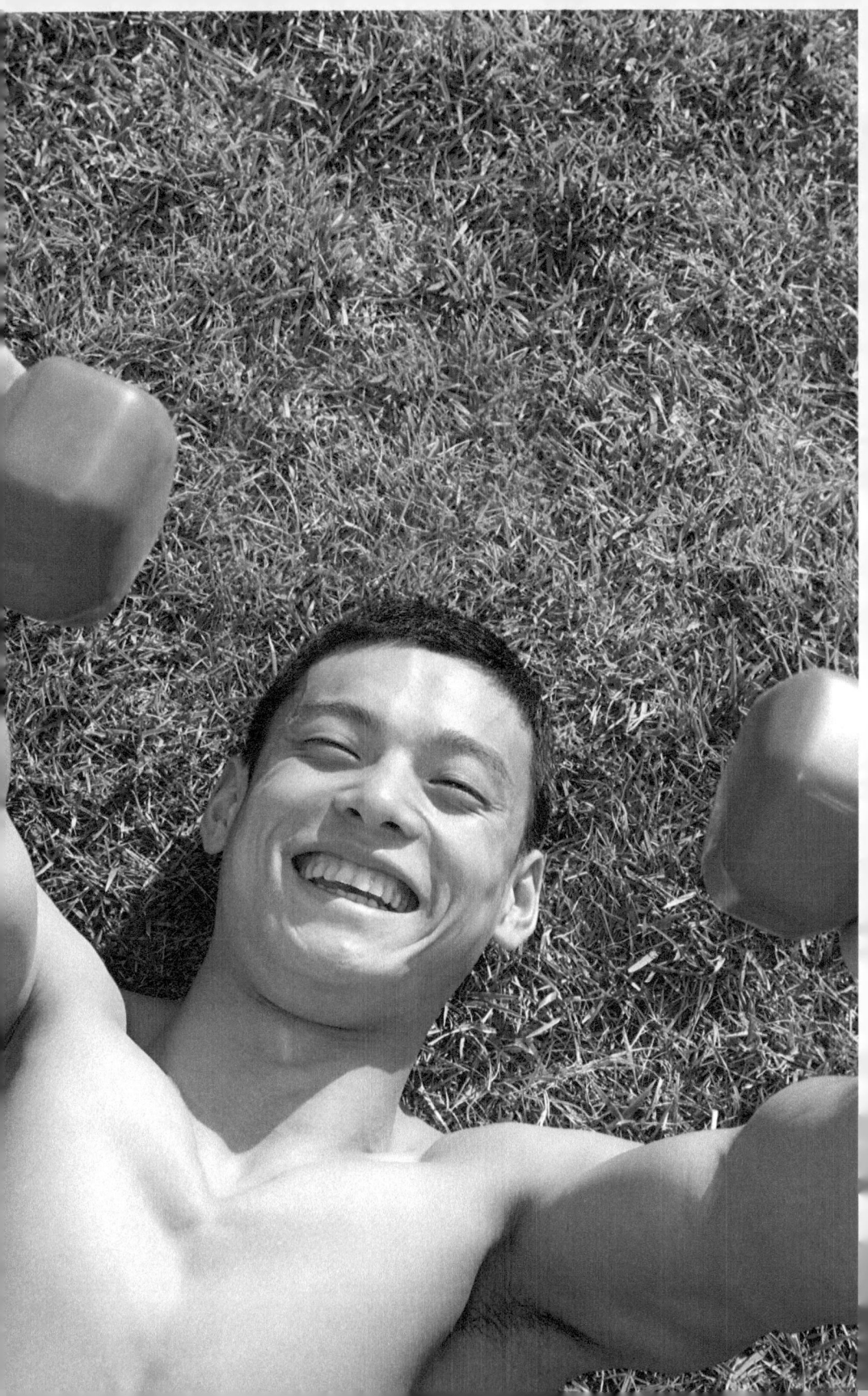

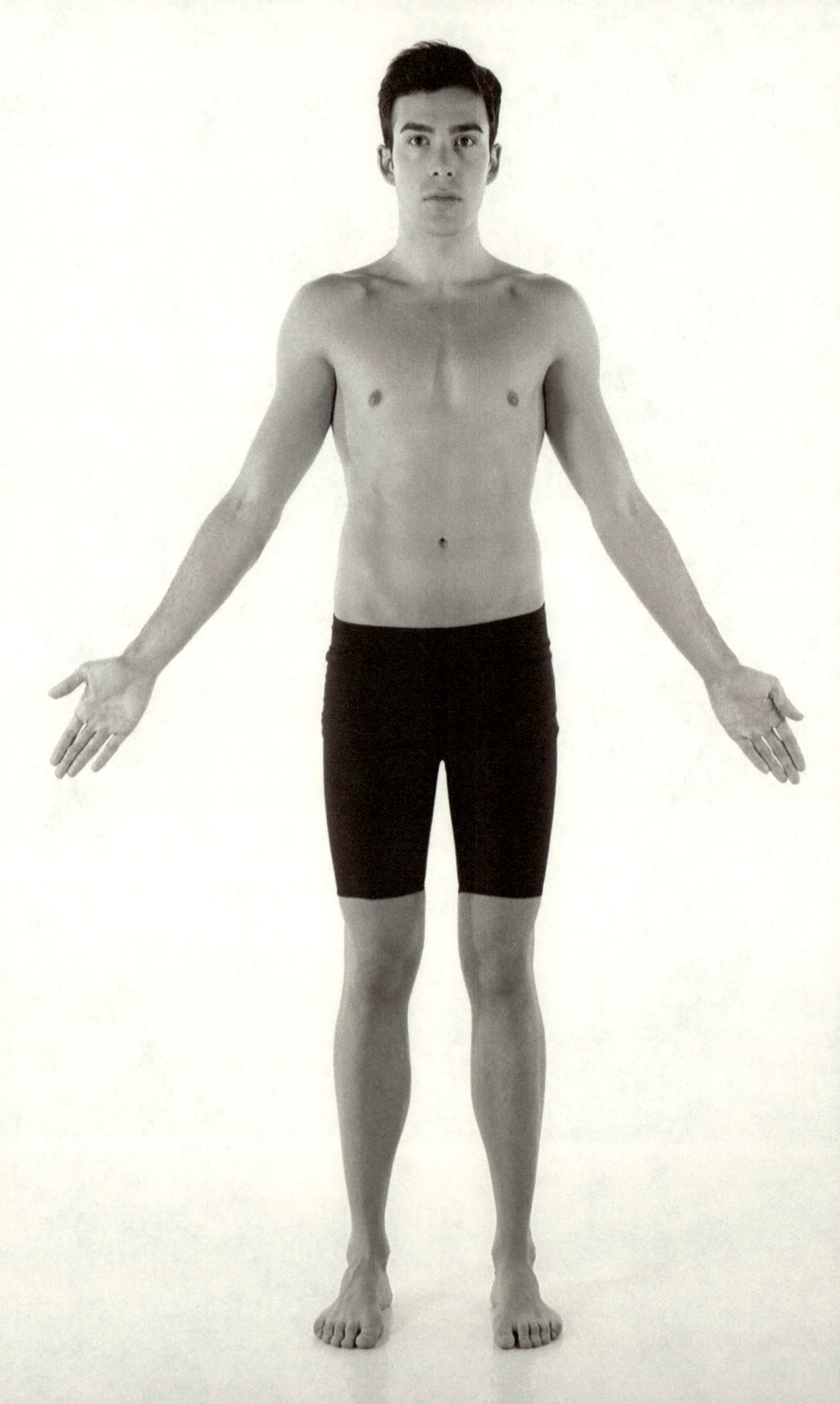

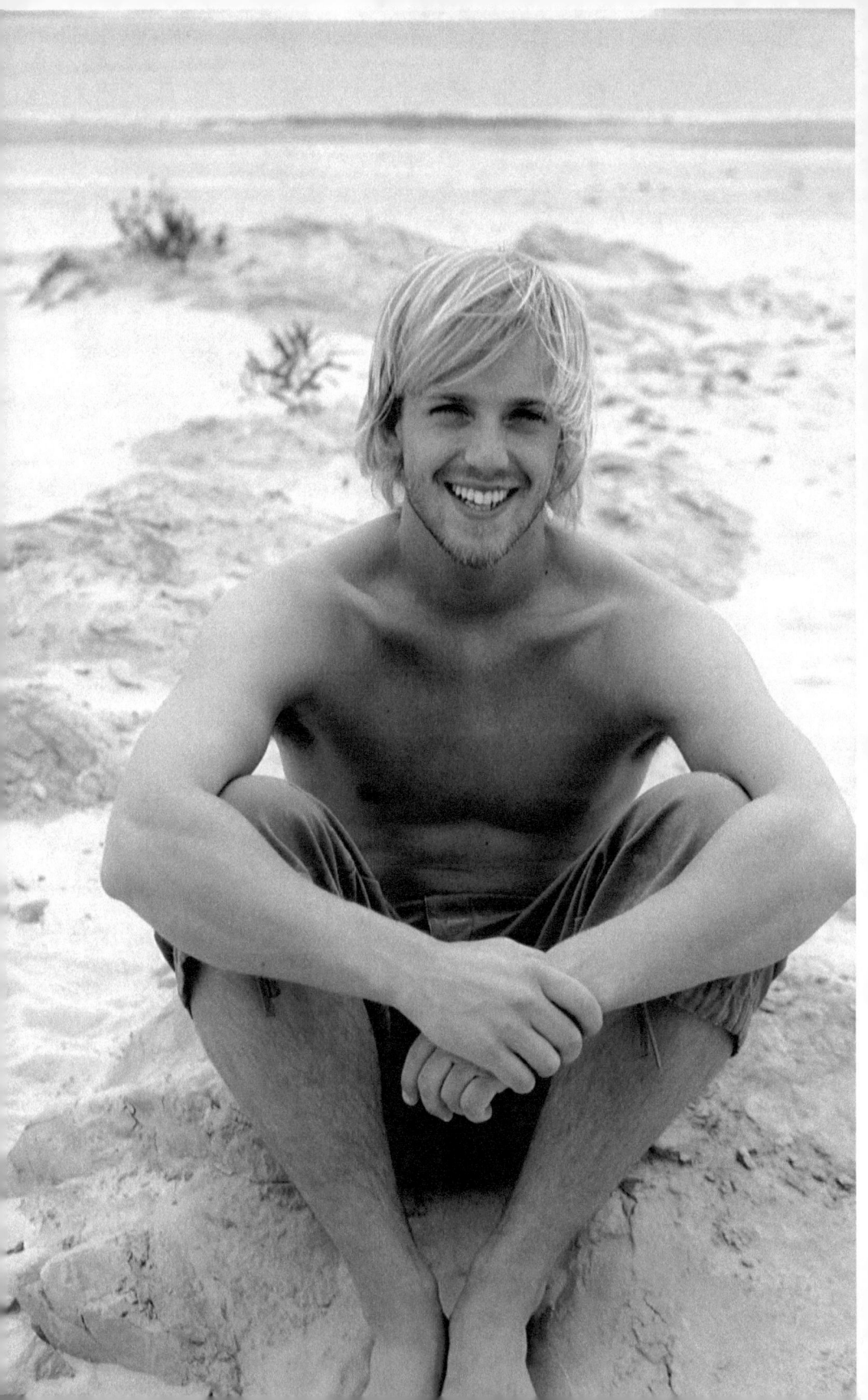

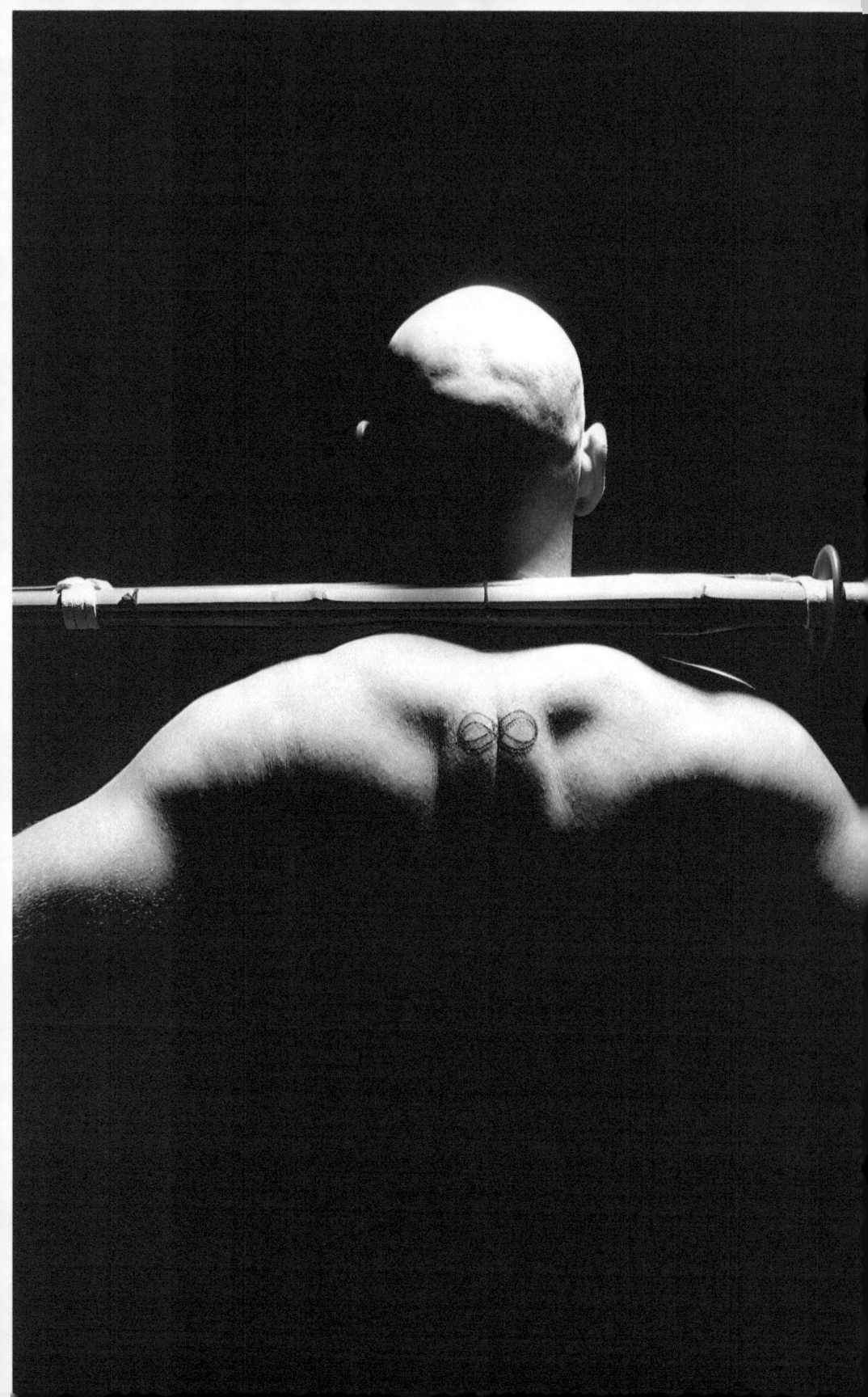

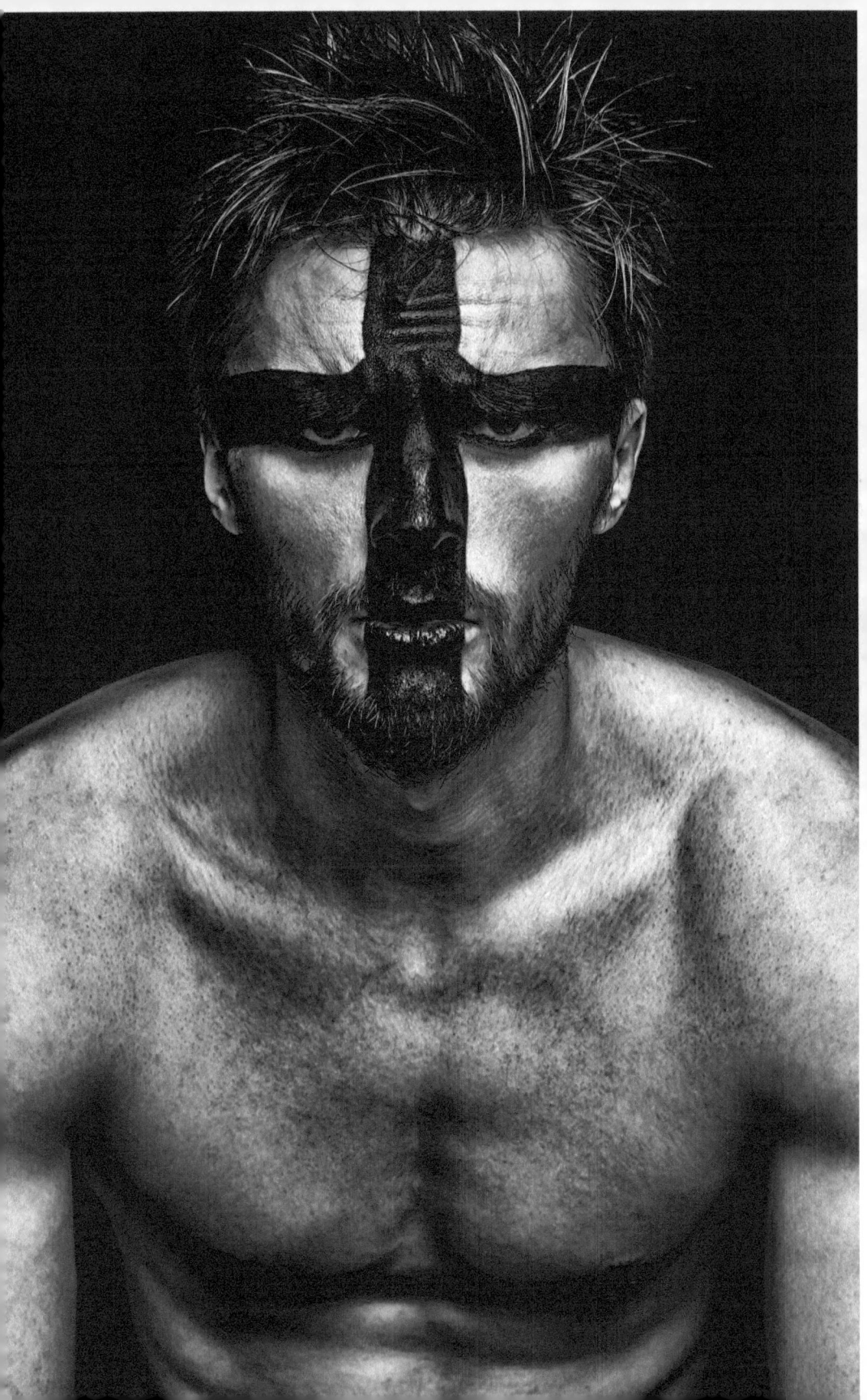

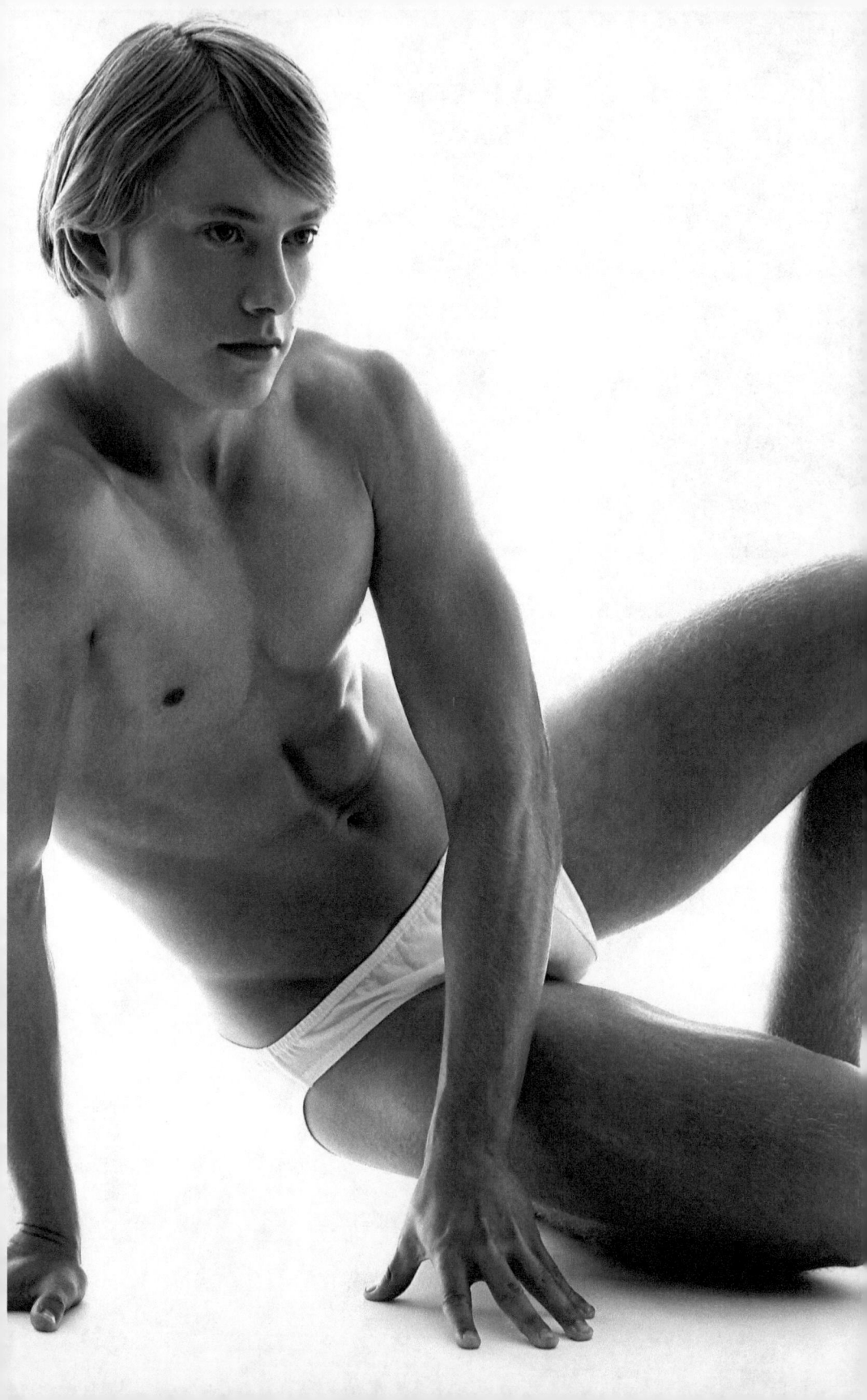

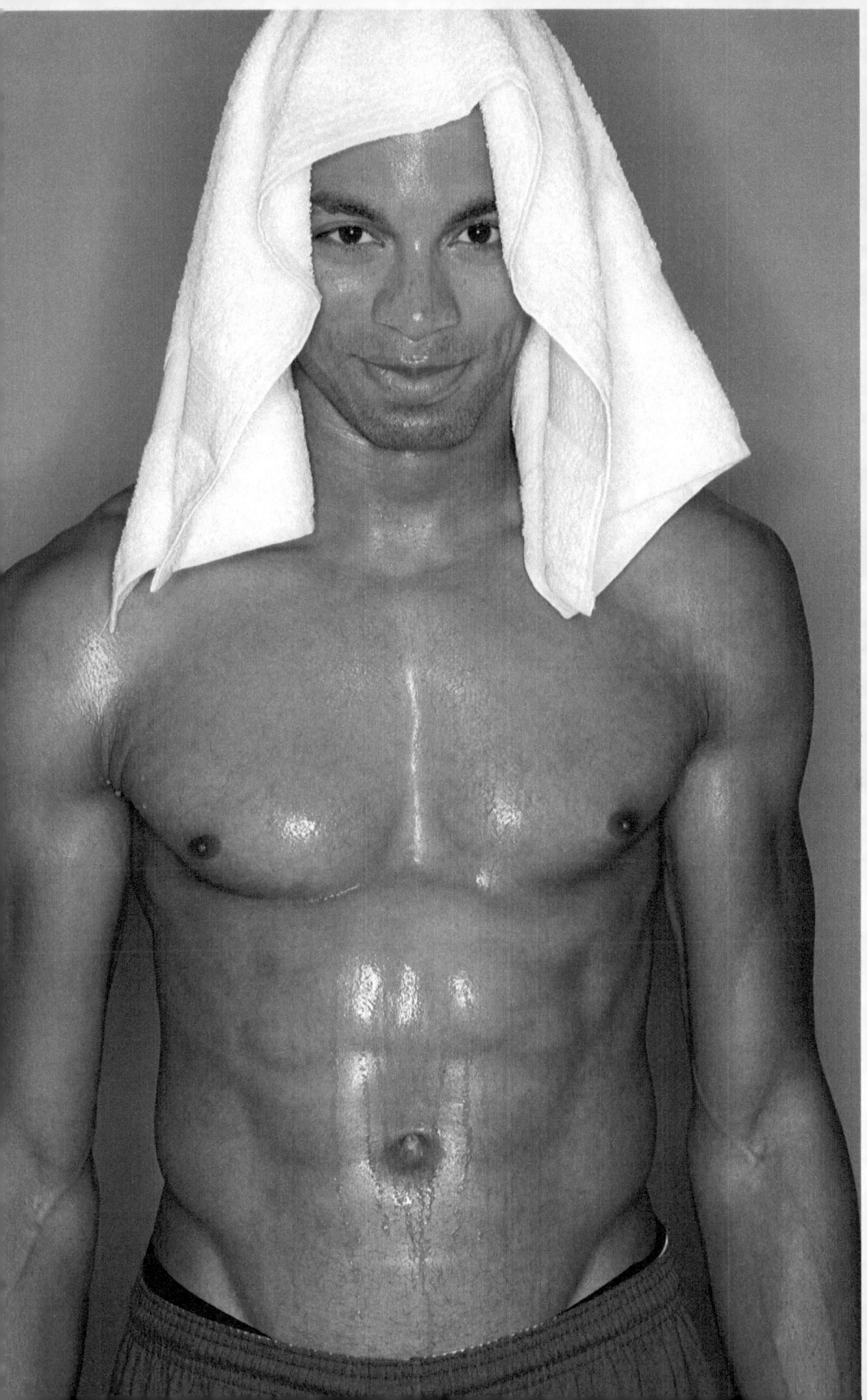

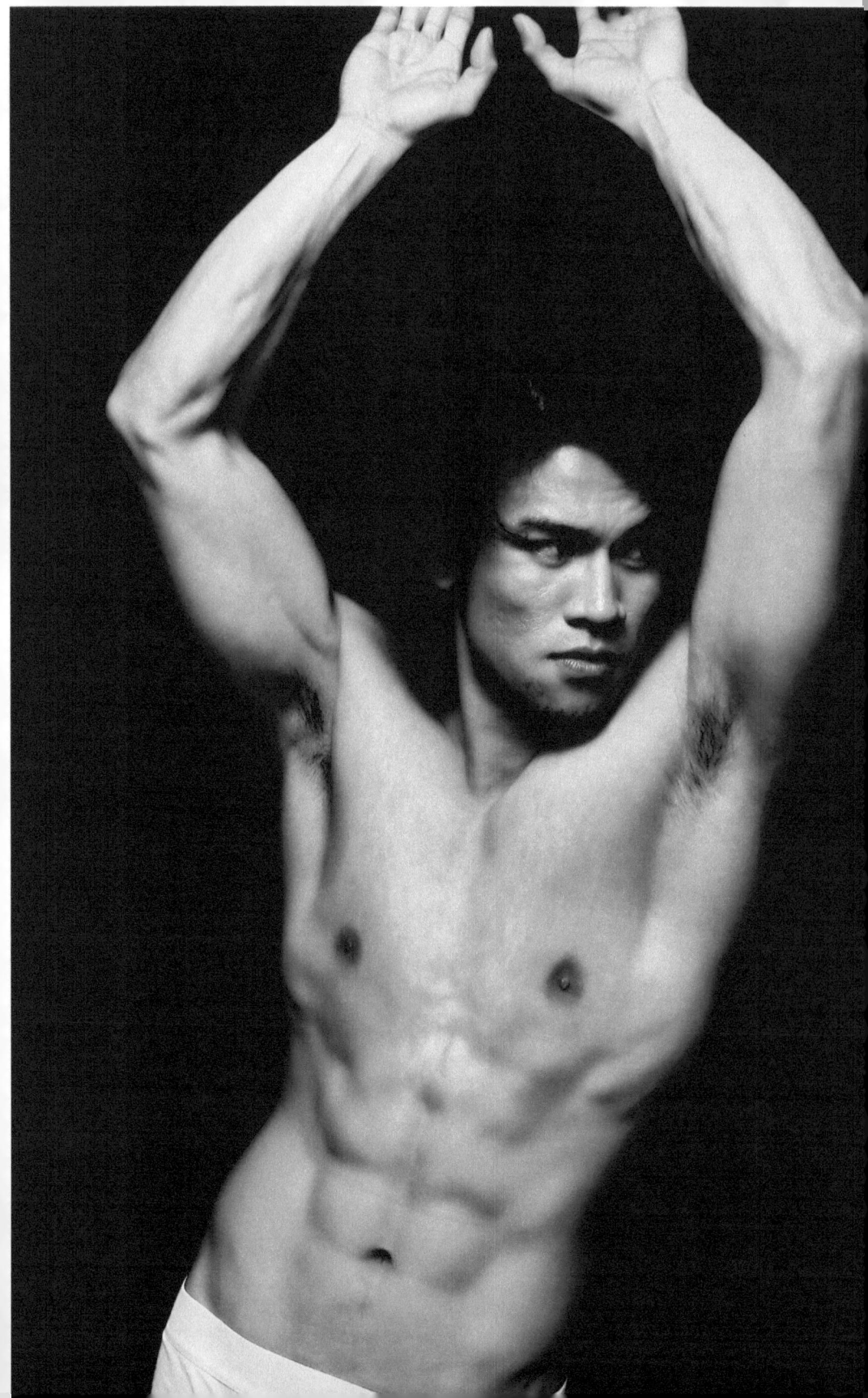

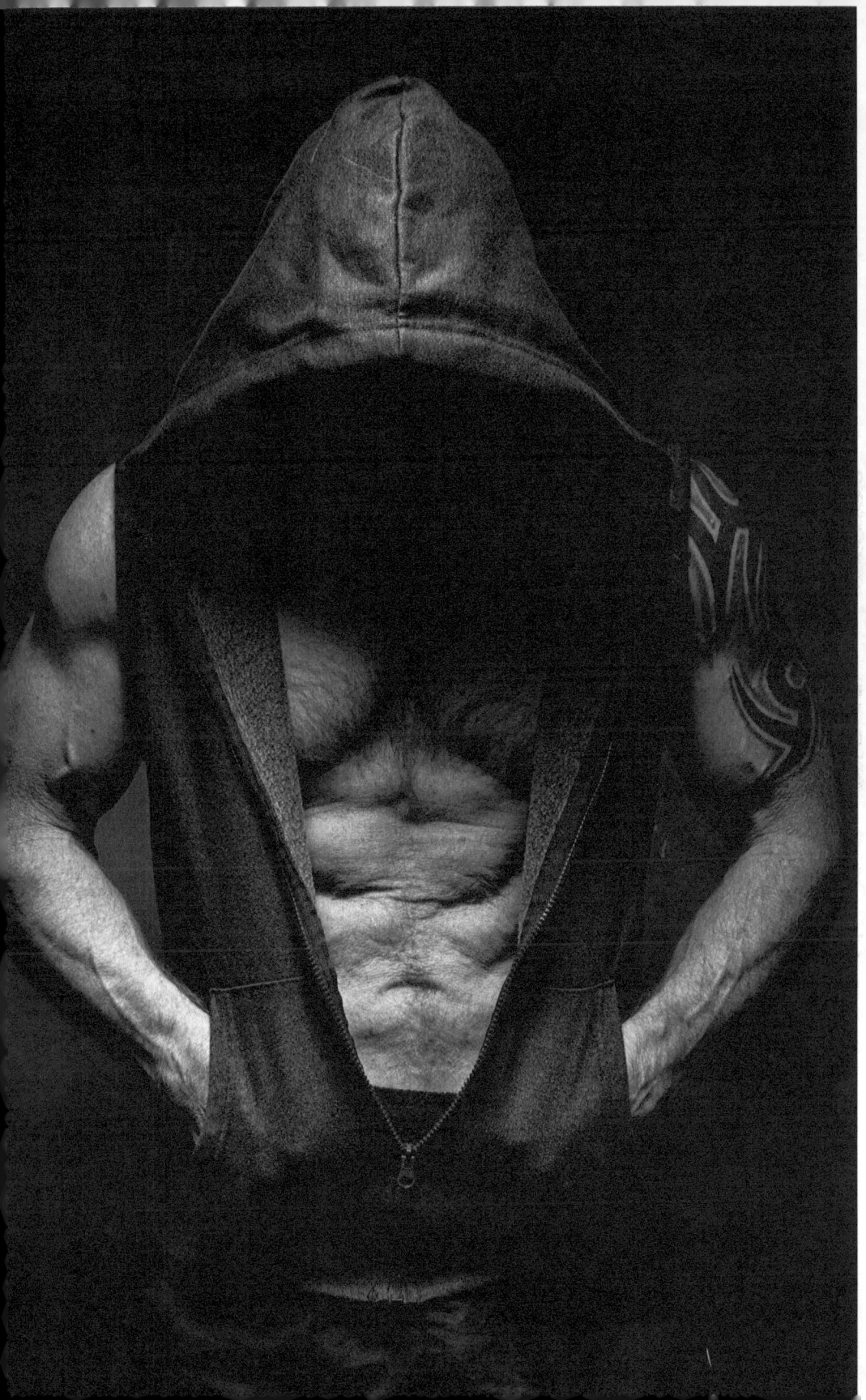

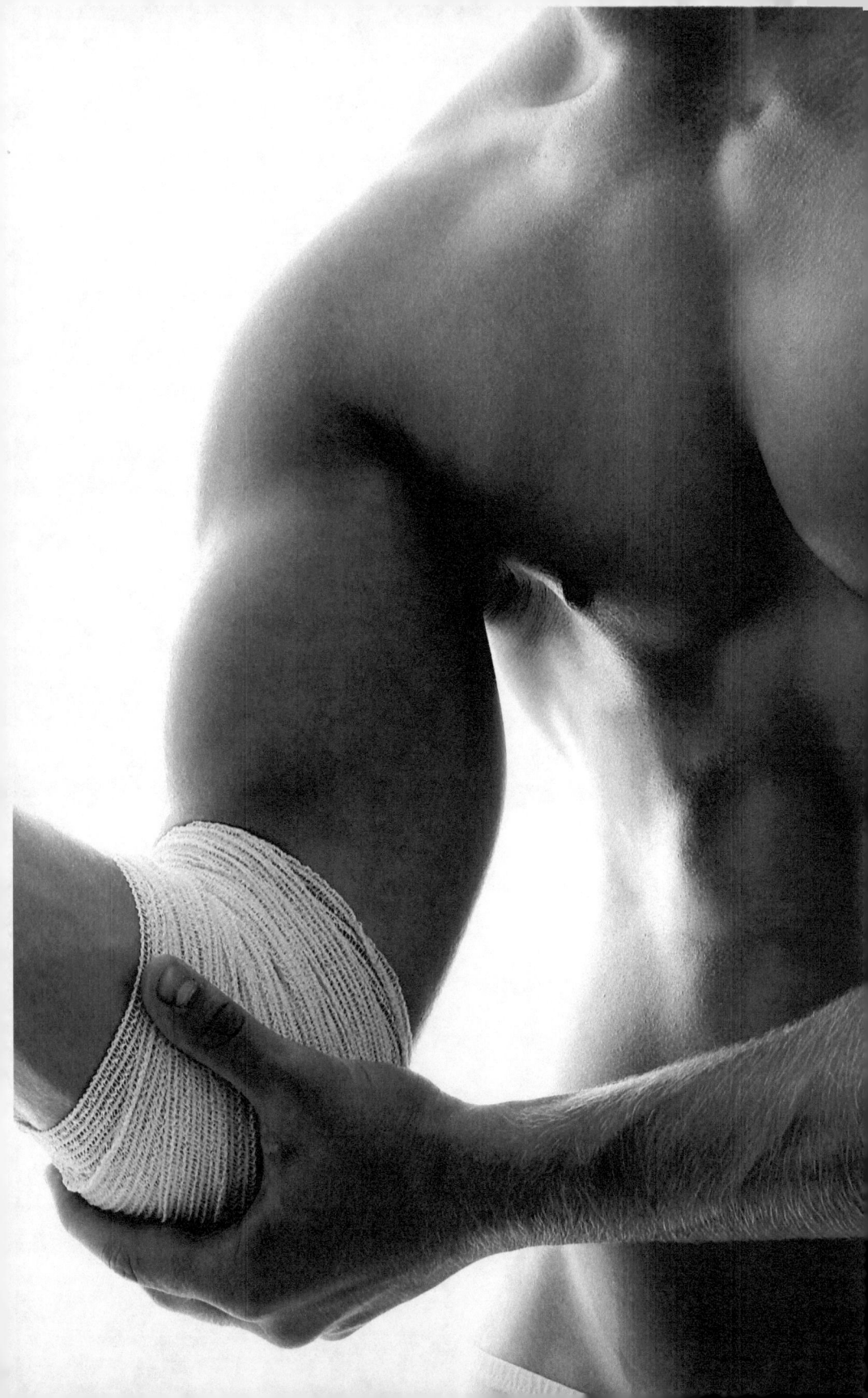

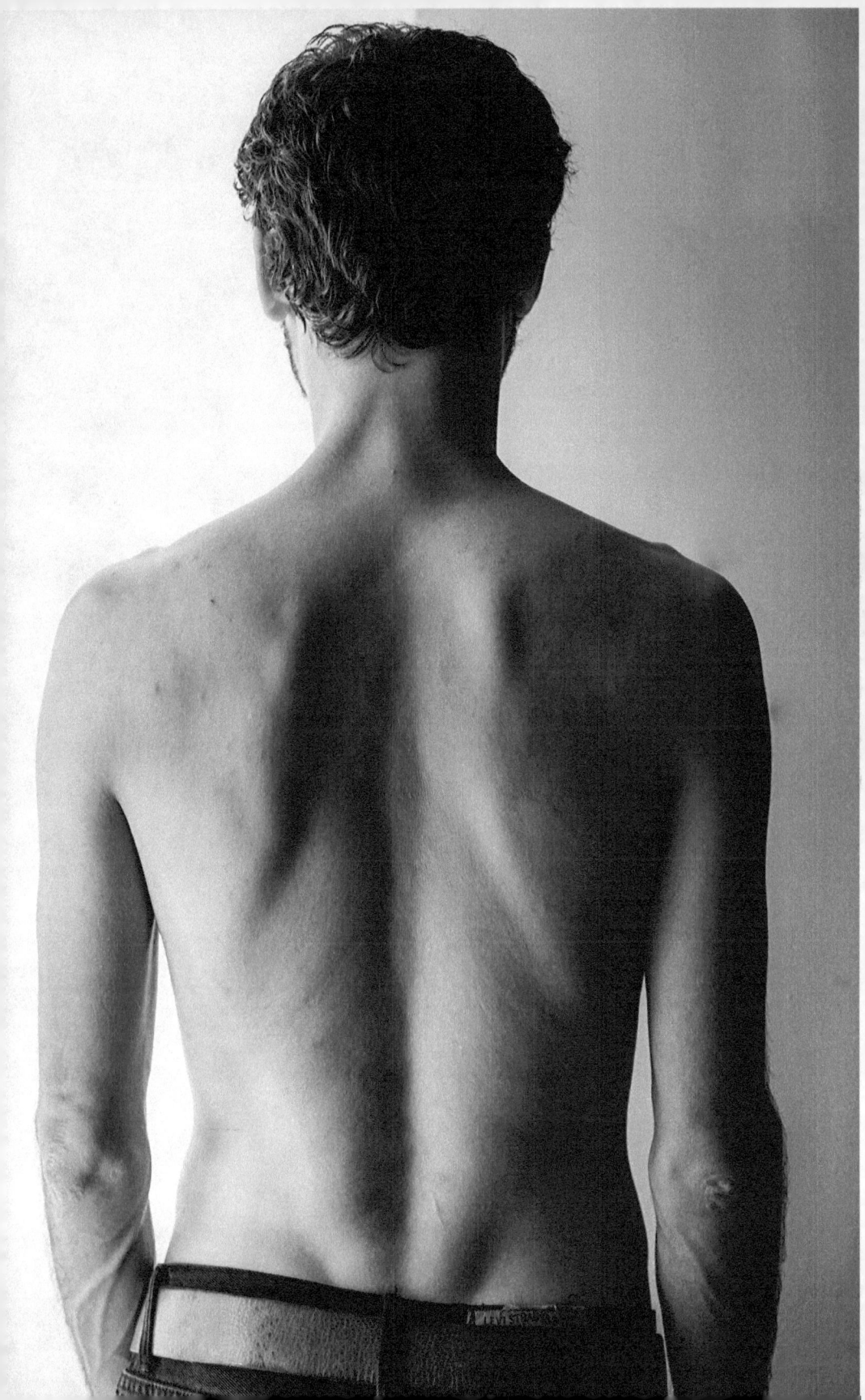

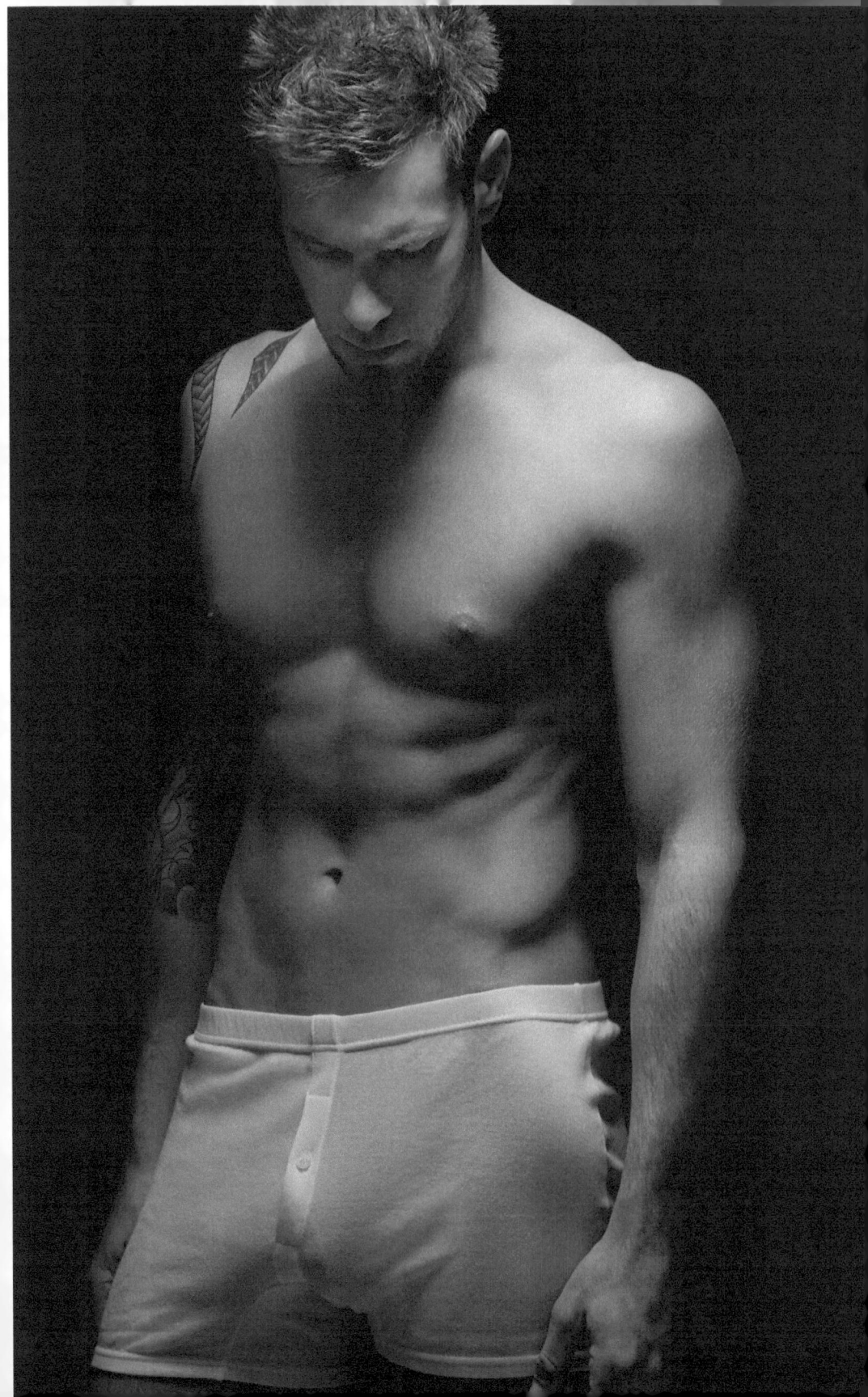

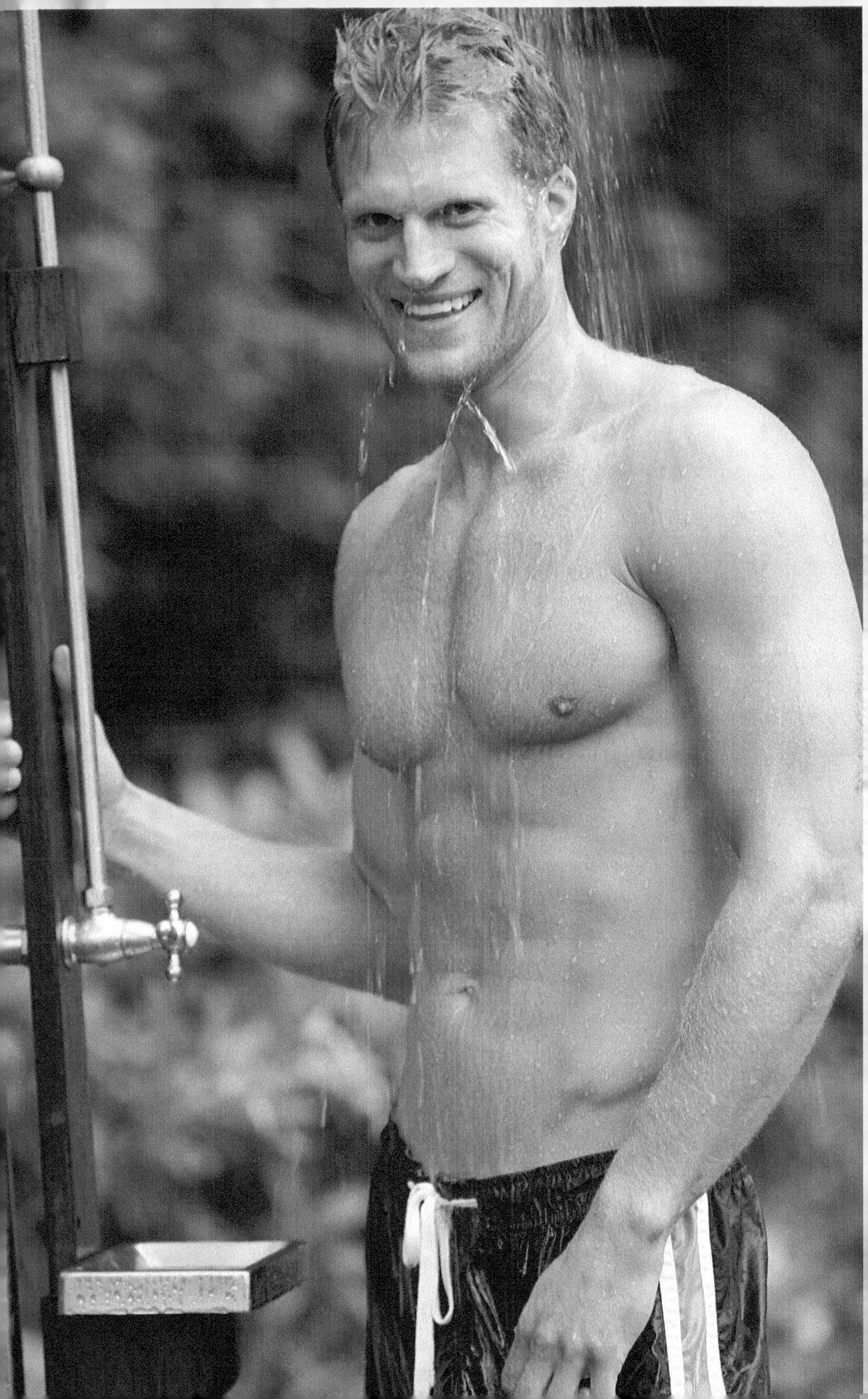

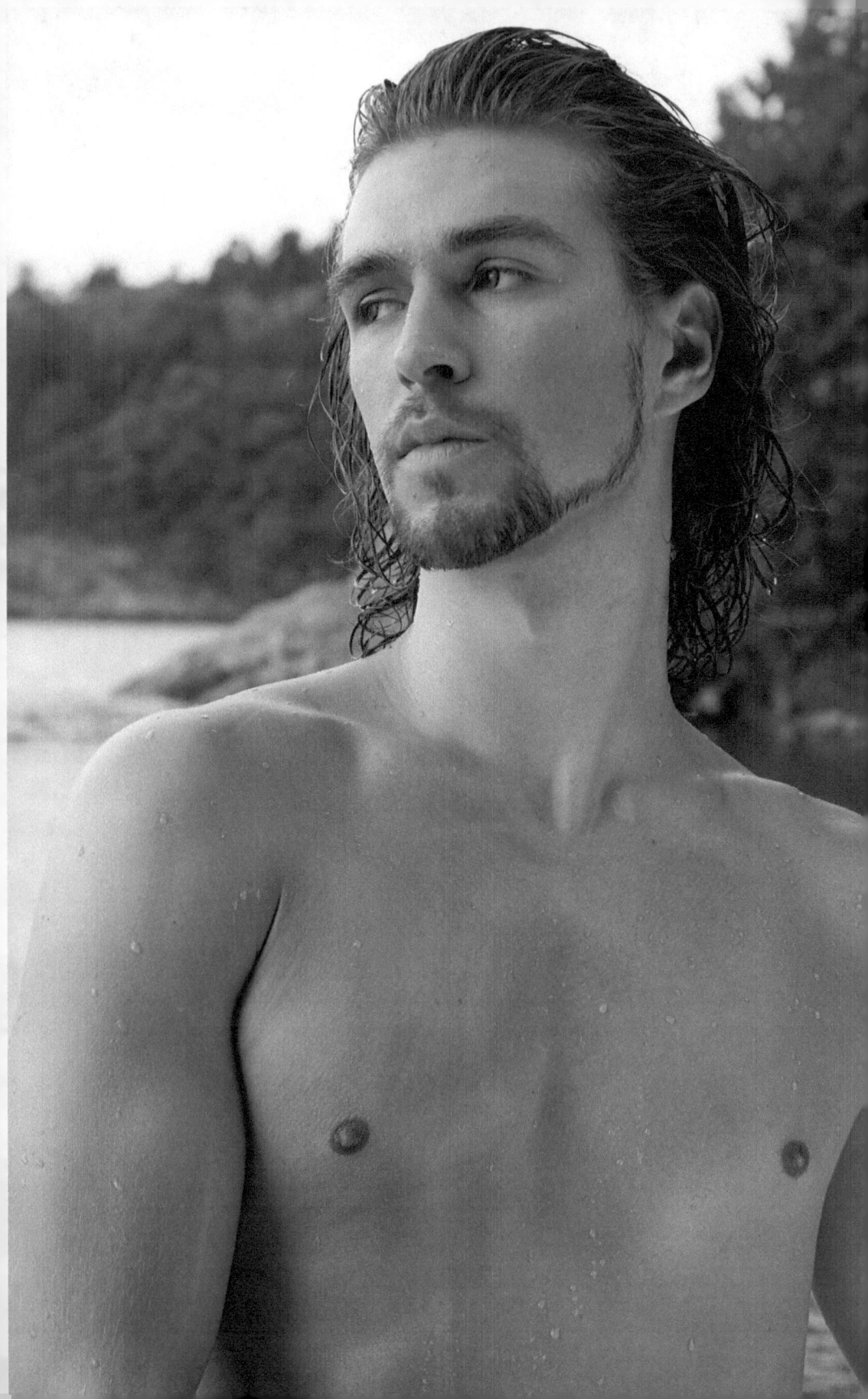

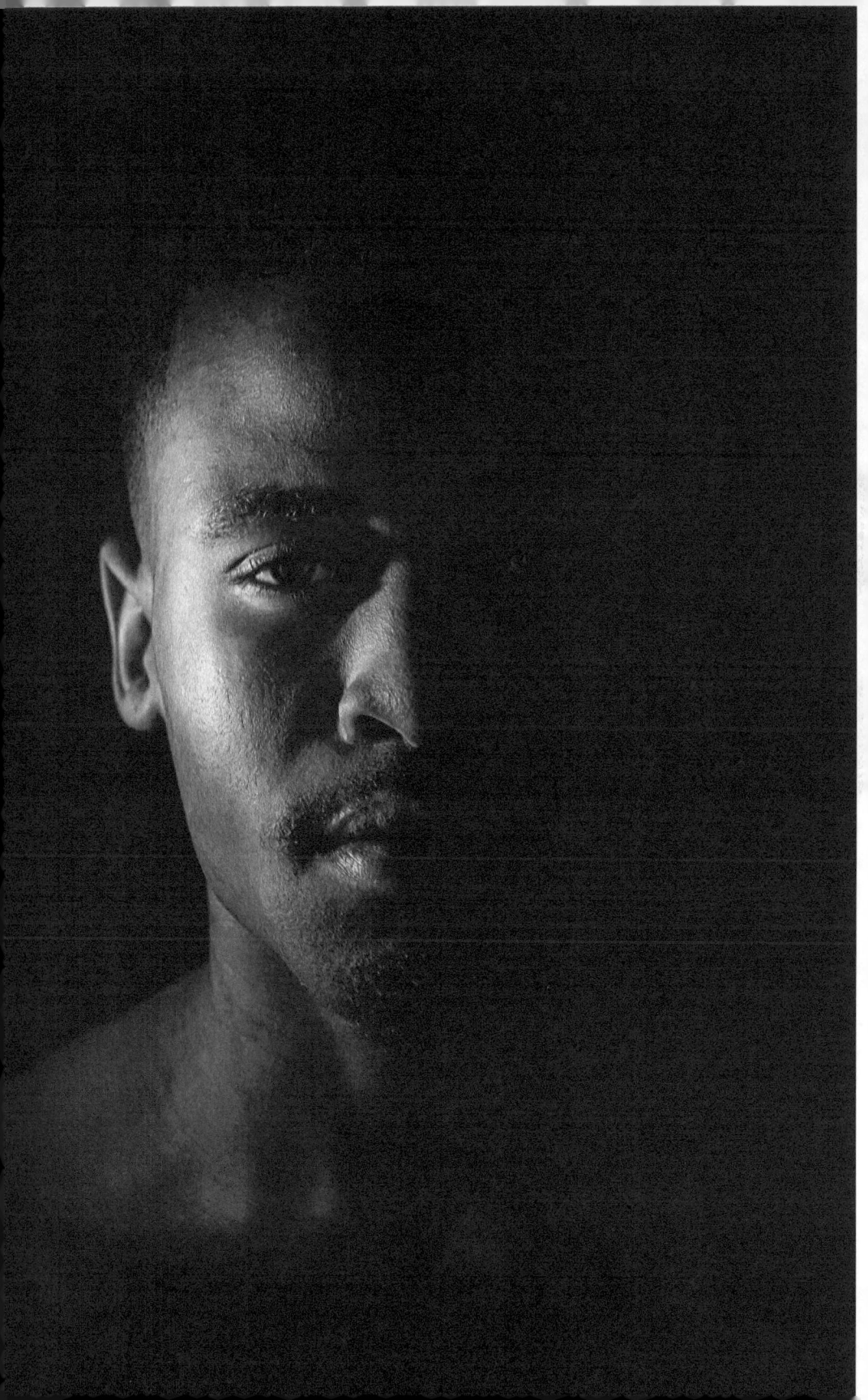

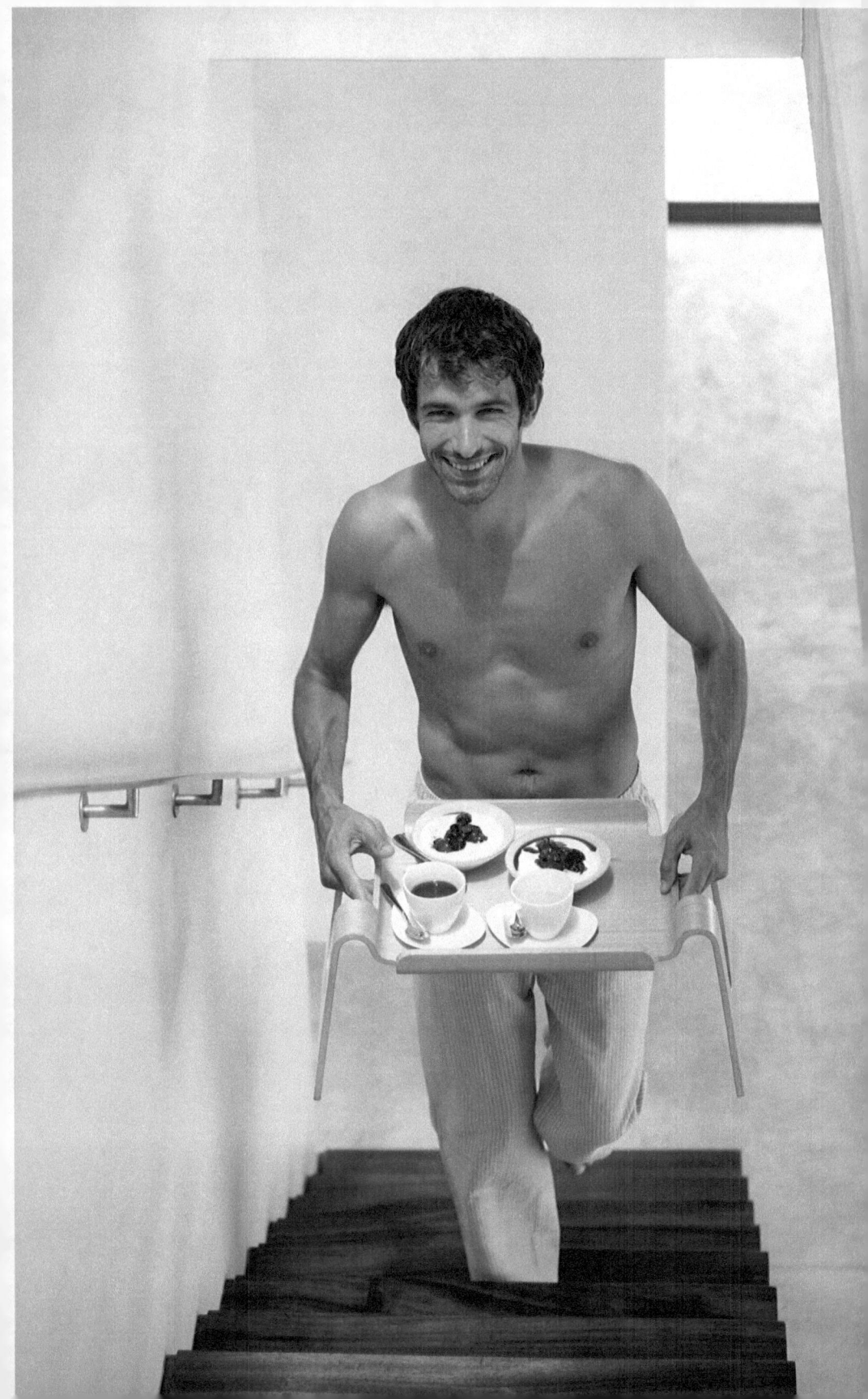

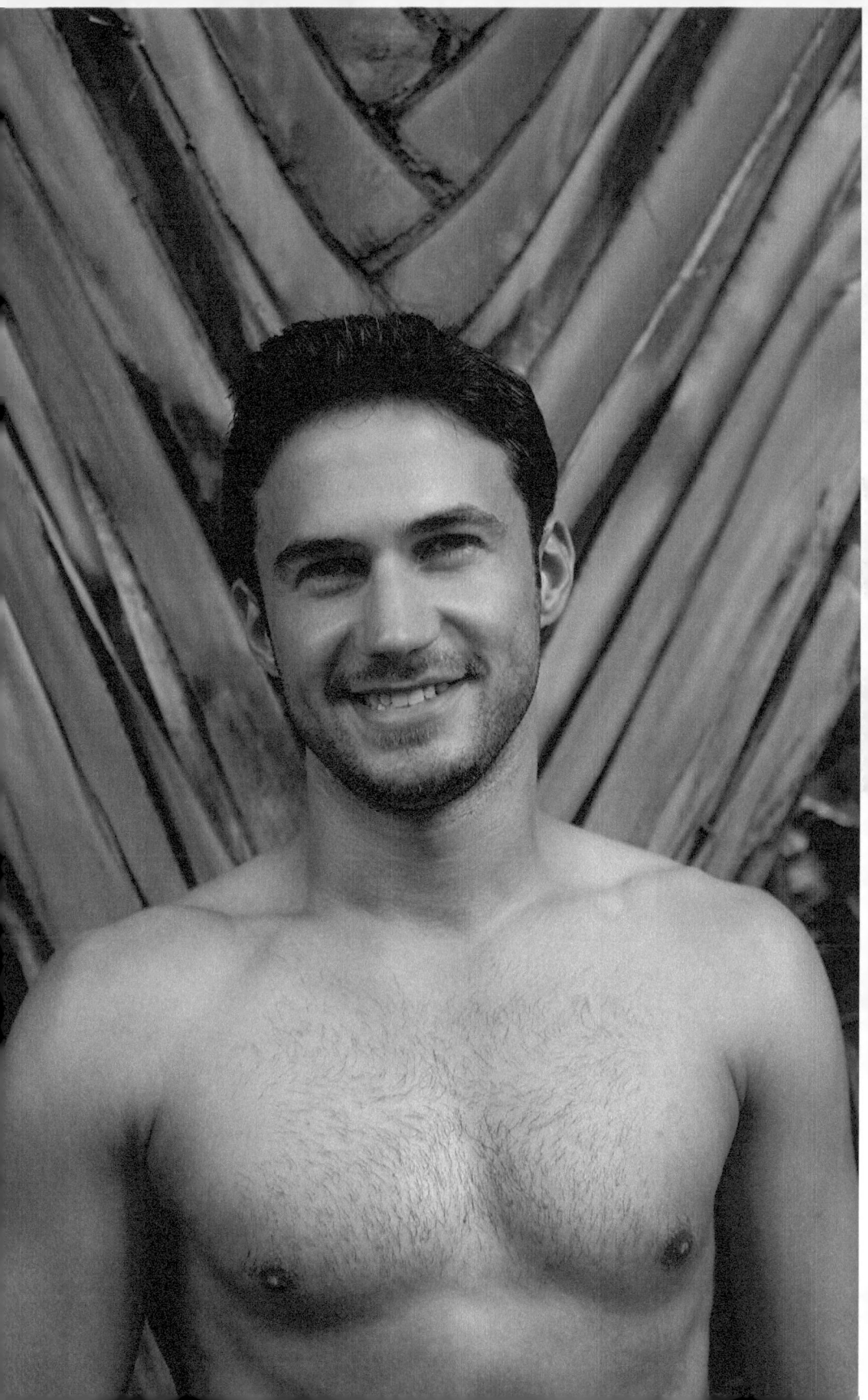

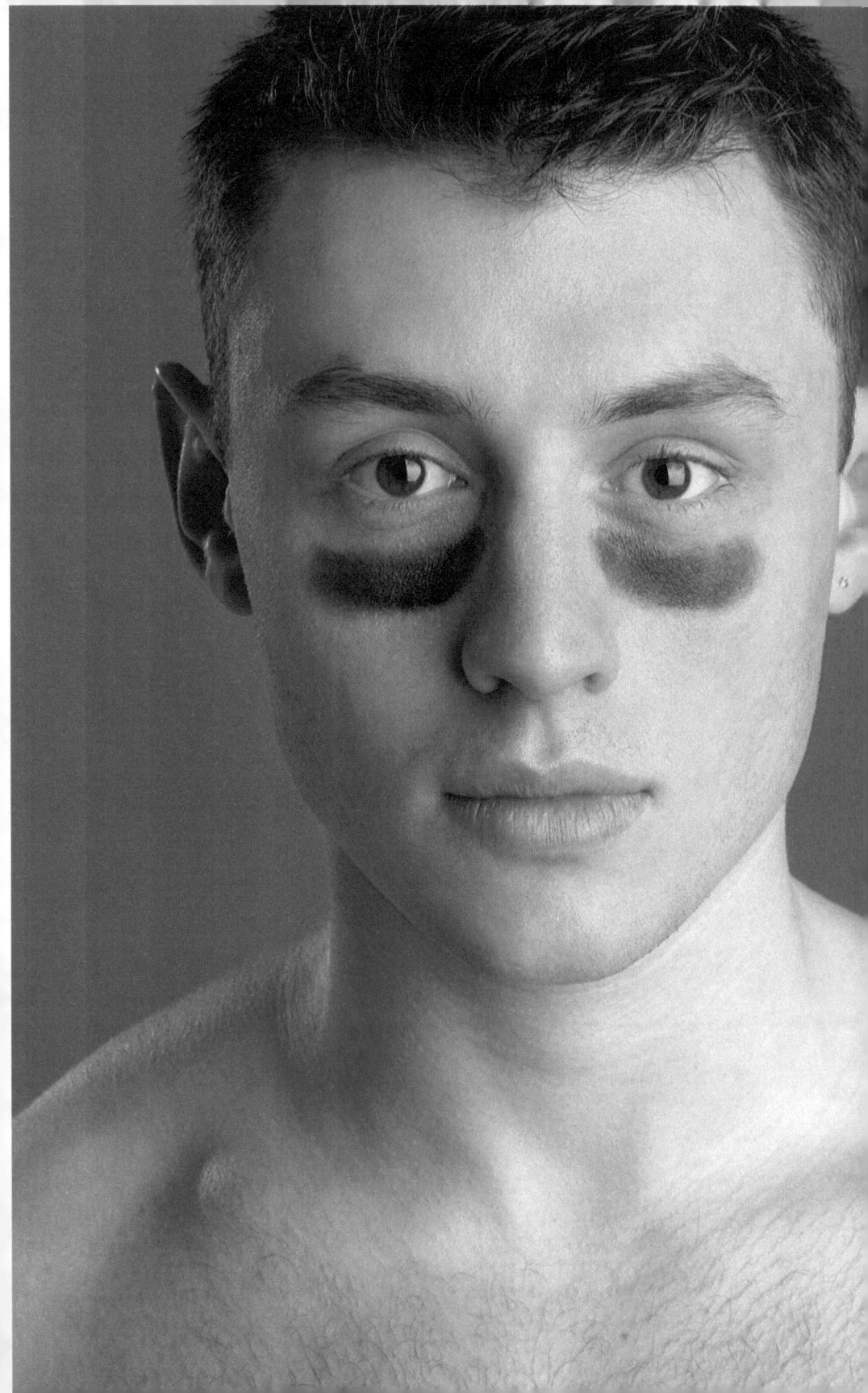

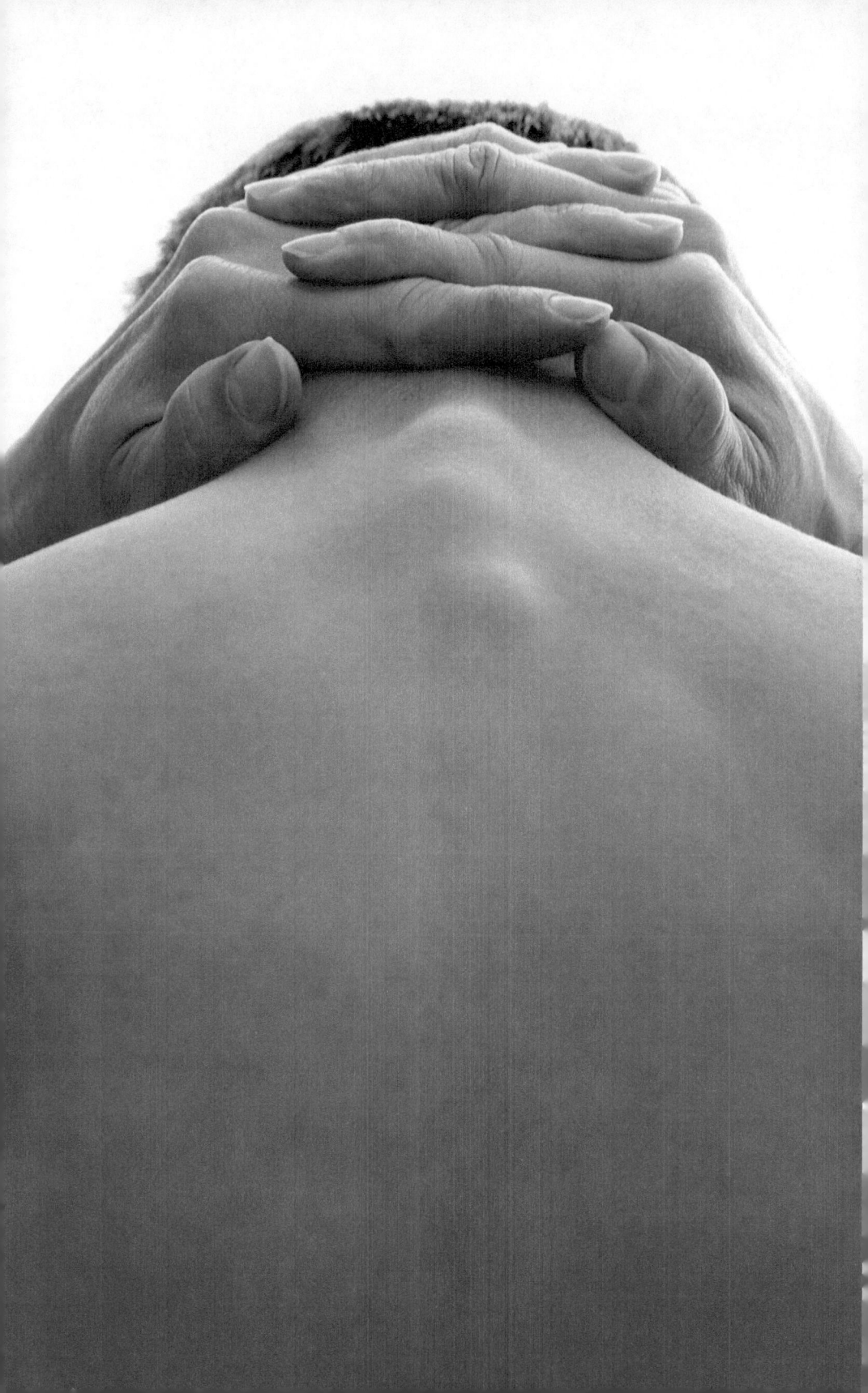

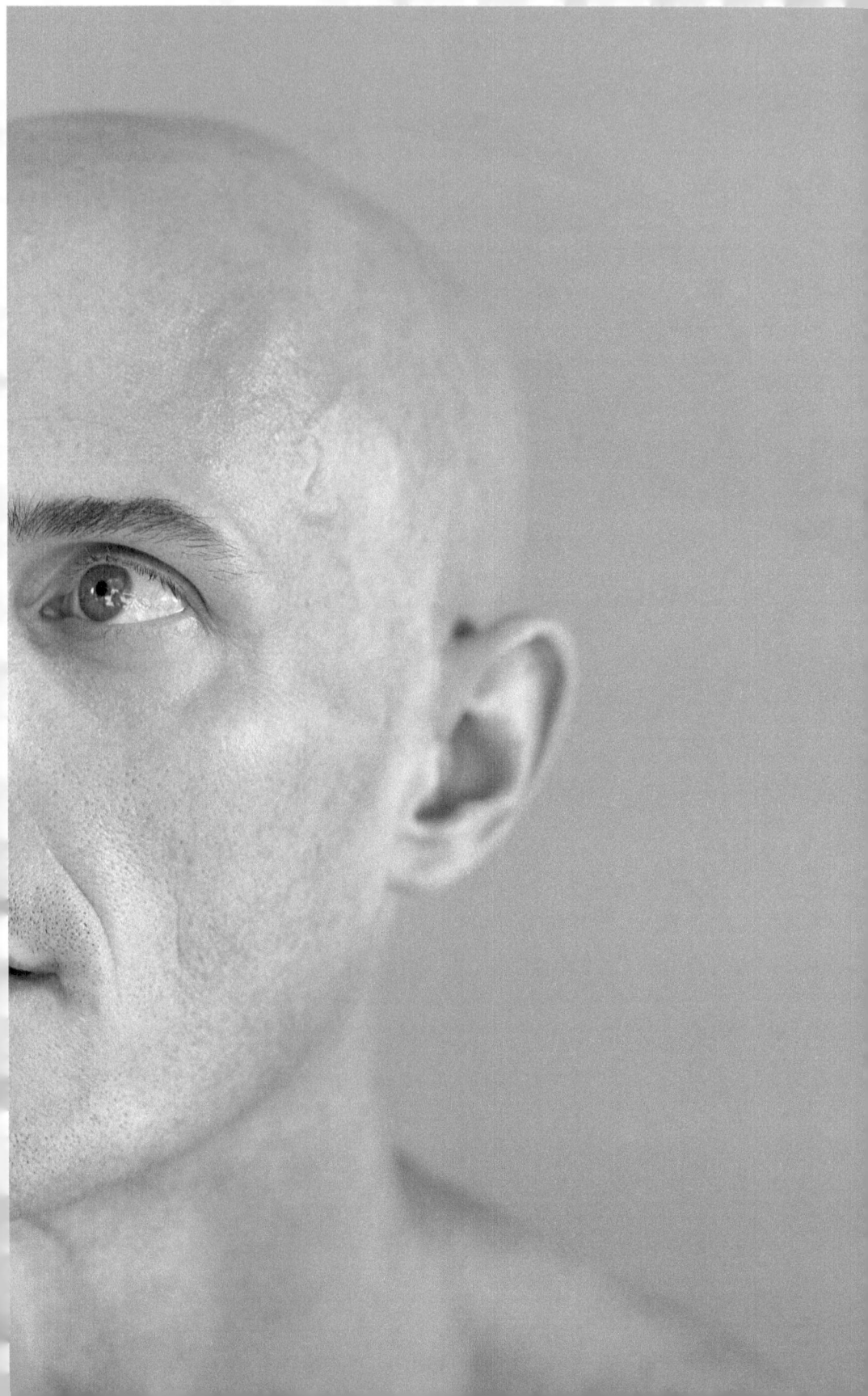

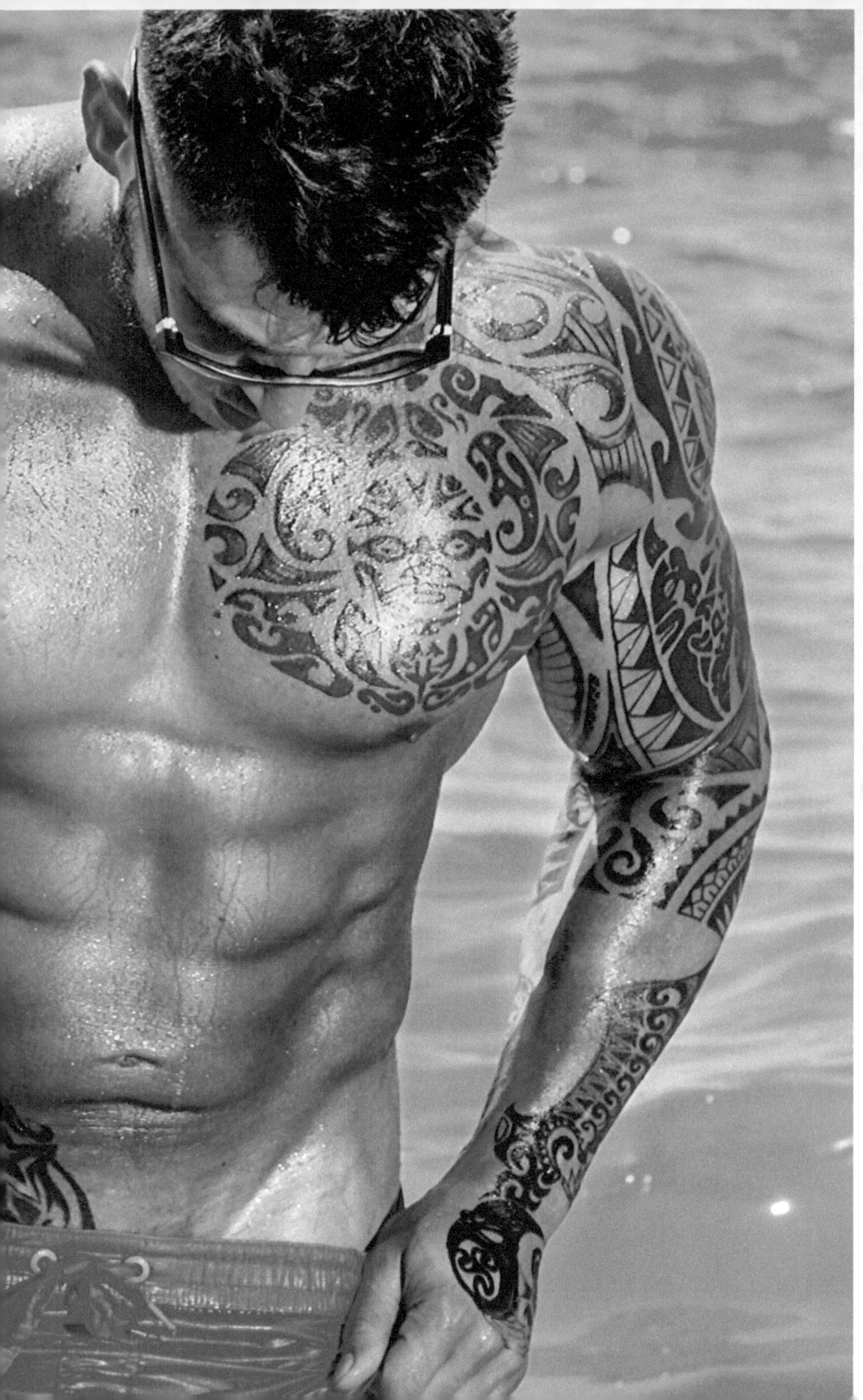

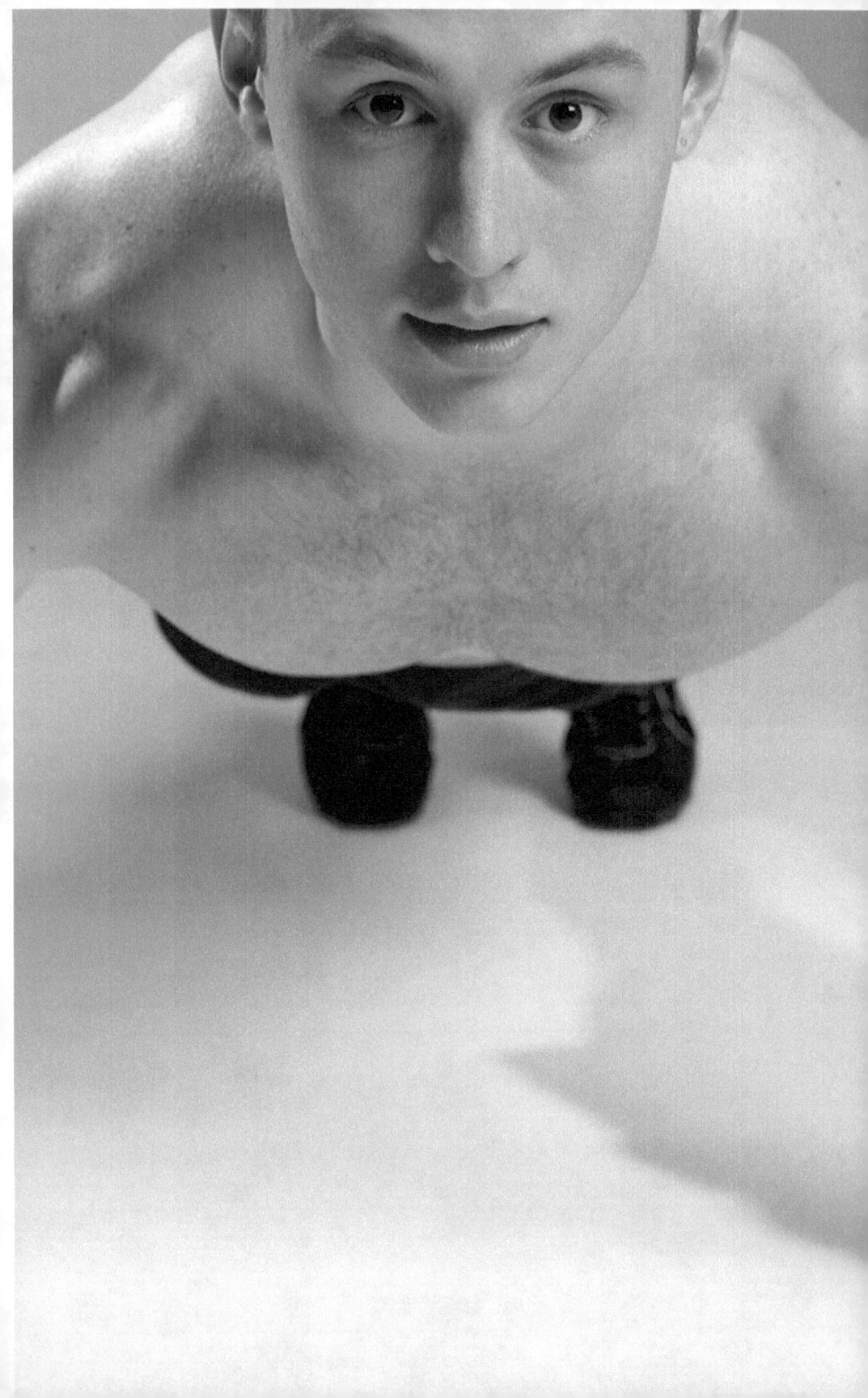

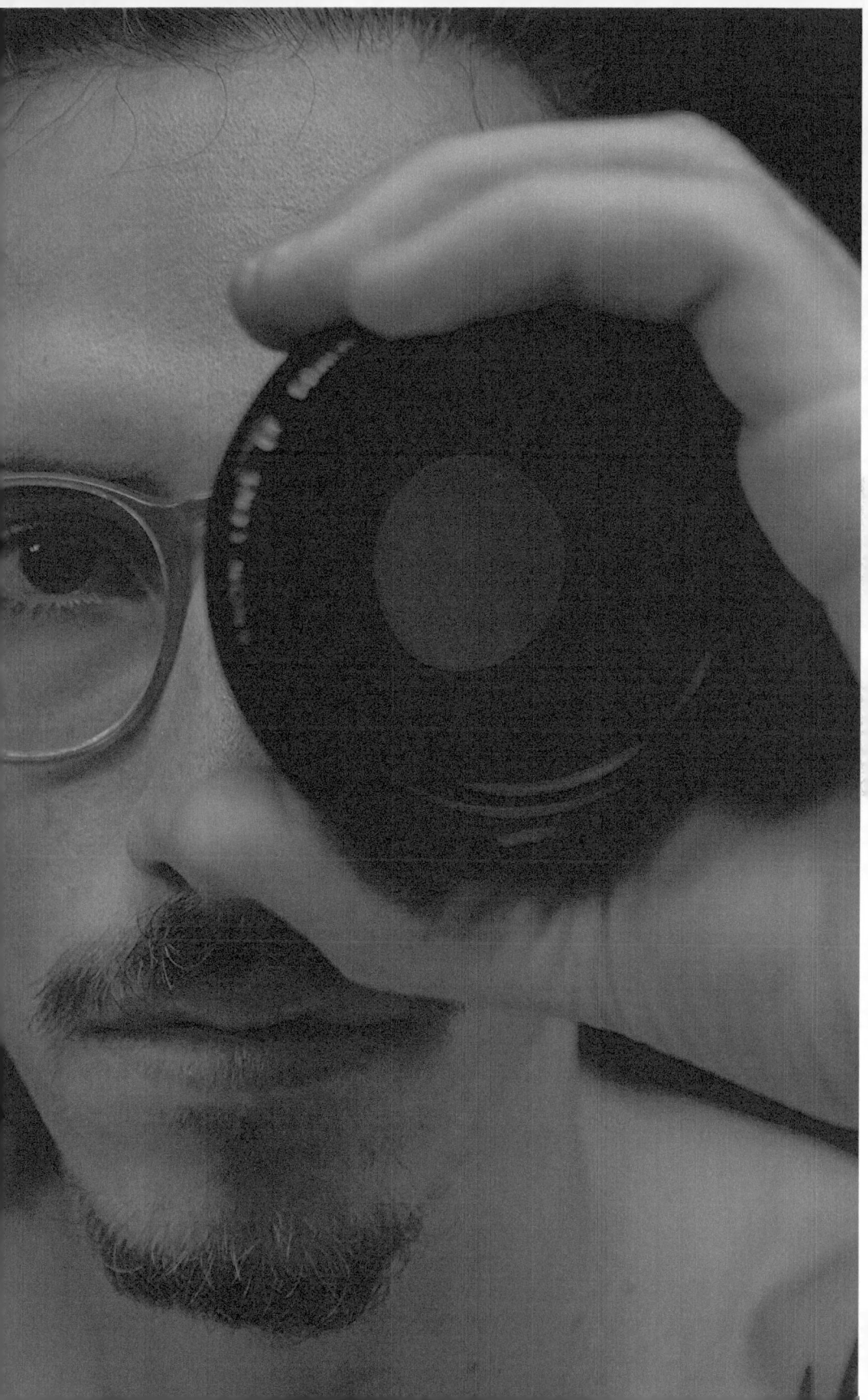

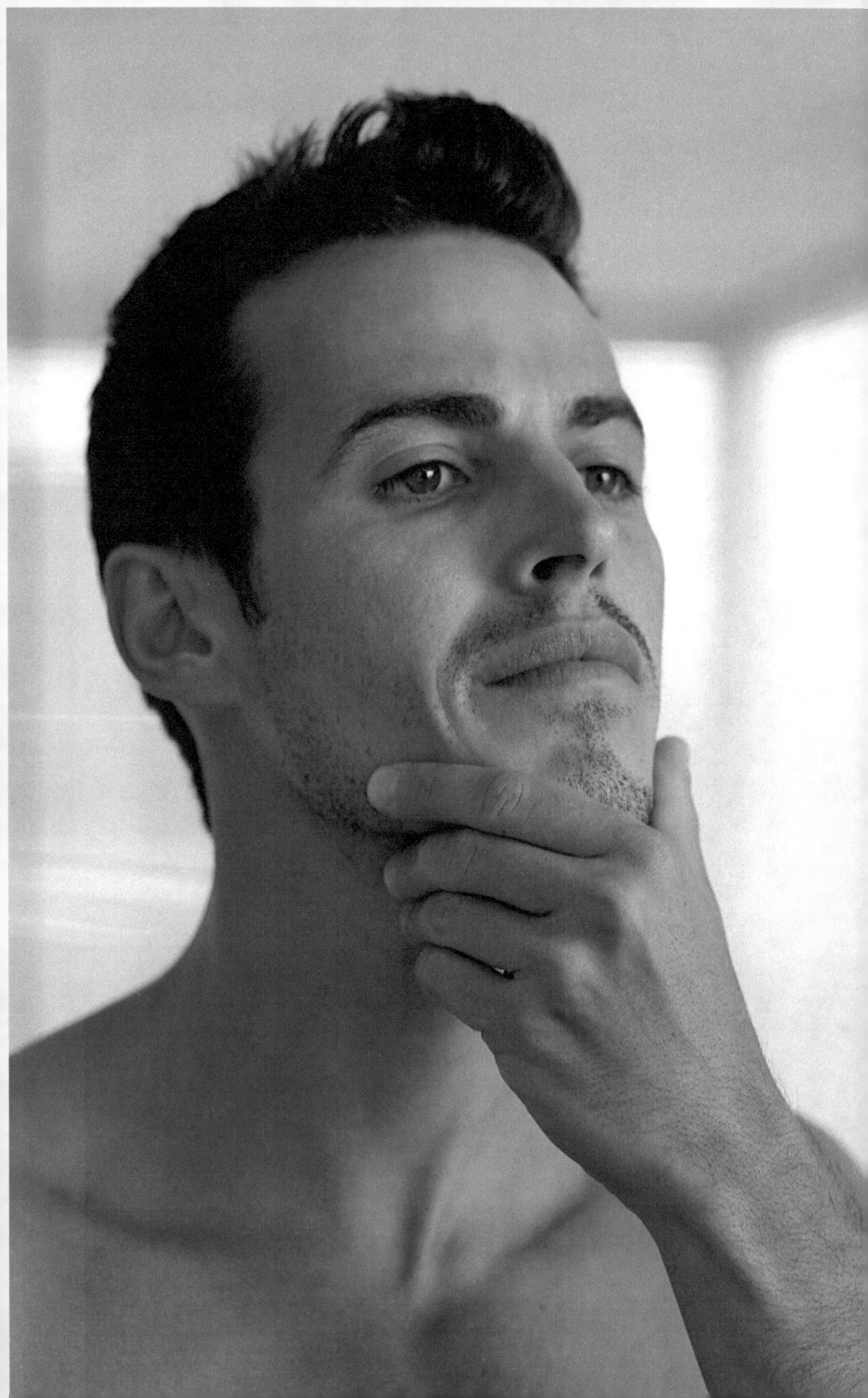

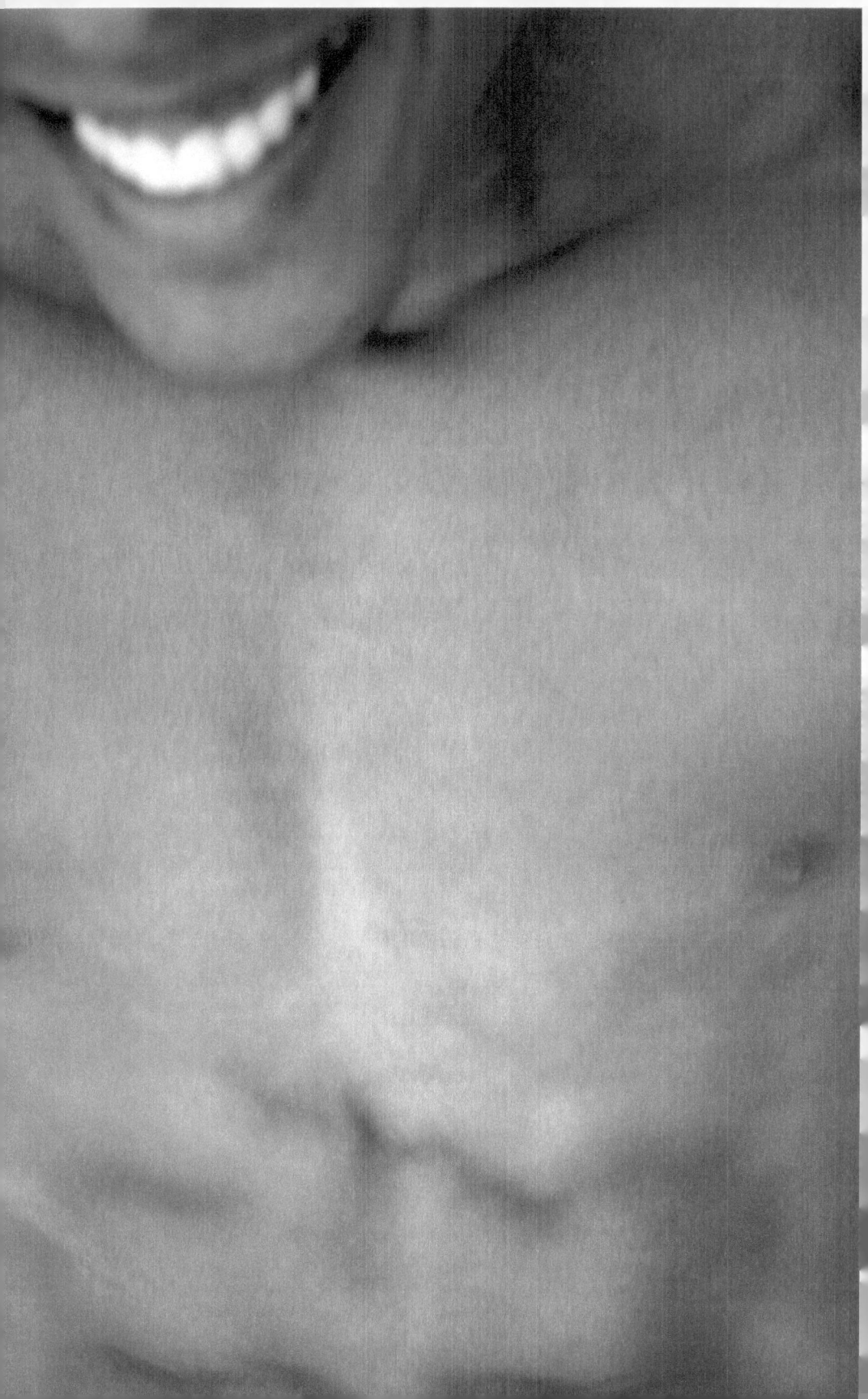

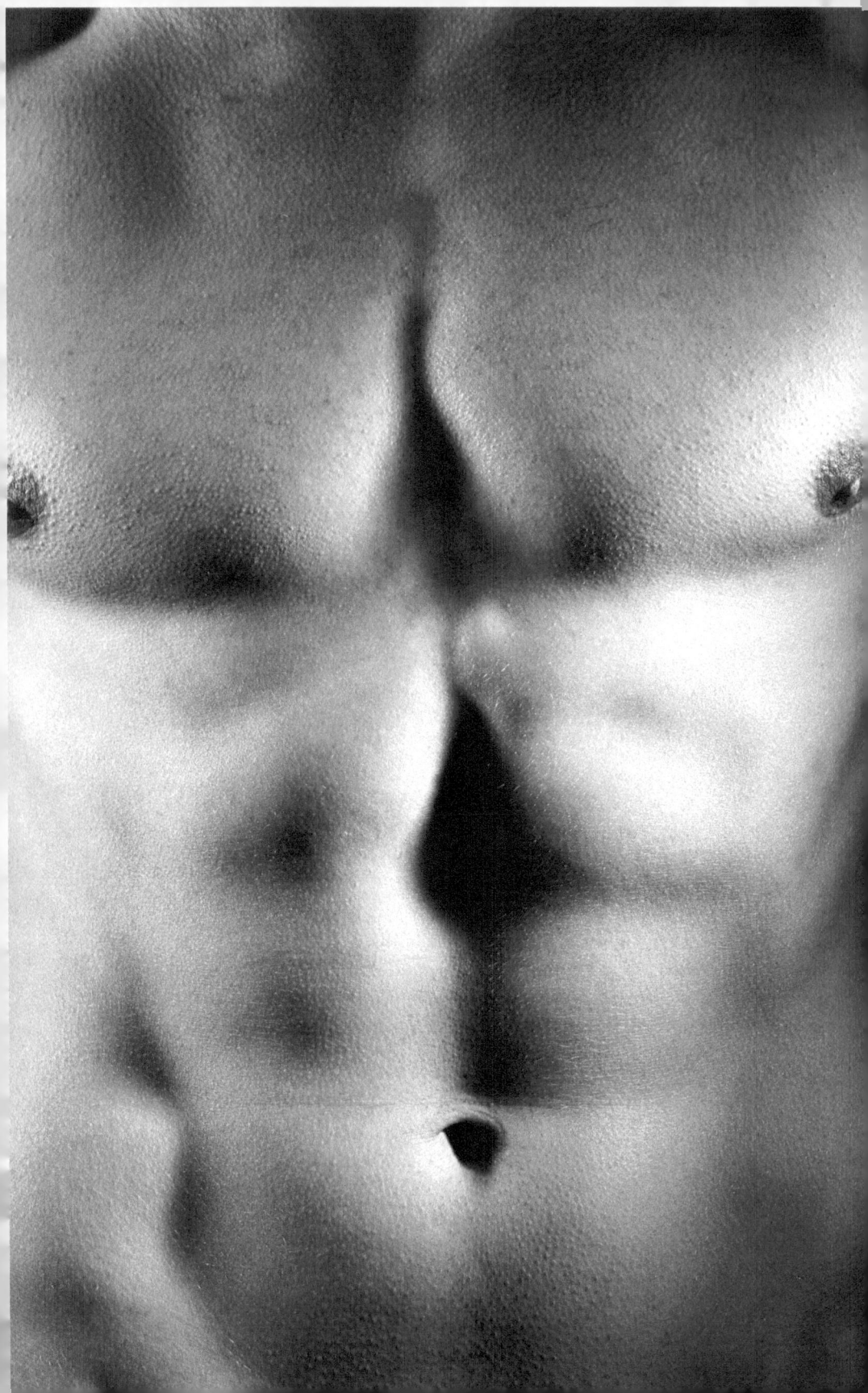

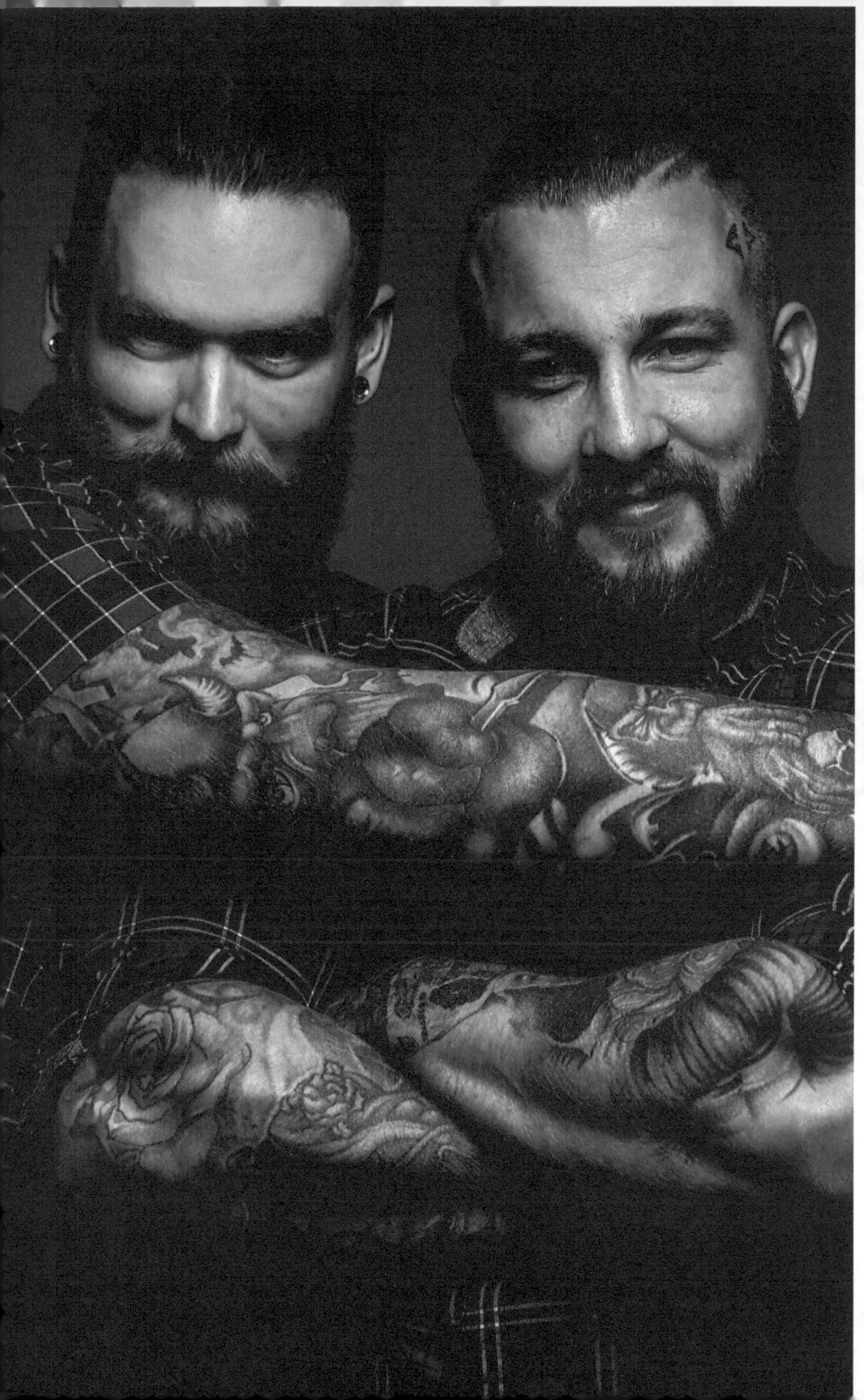

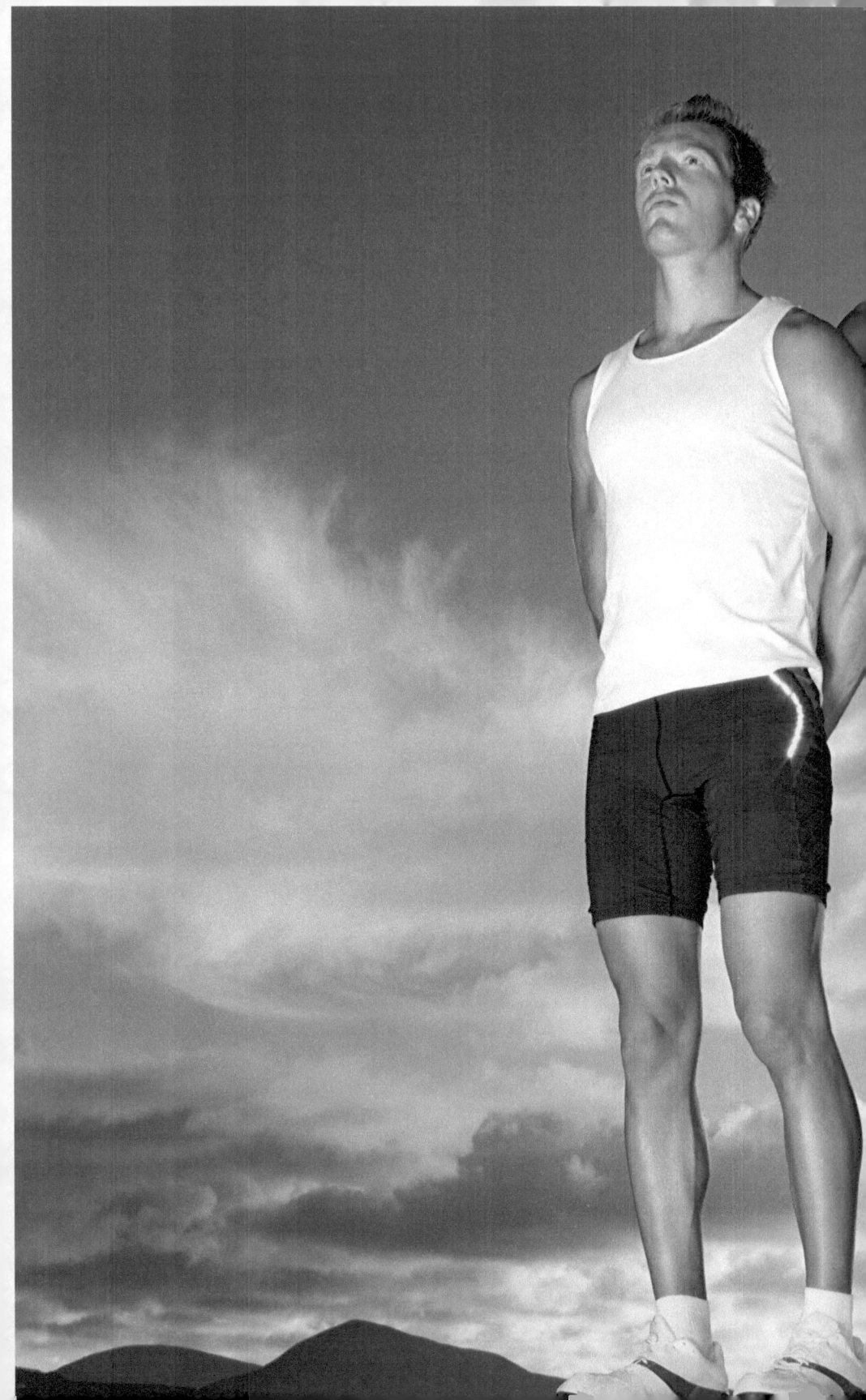

www.ingramcontent.com/pod-product-compliance
Lightning Source LLC
Chambersburg PA
CBHW030907180526
45163CB00004B/1748